T0159131

1001 IDIOMS
TO MASTER YOUR ENGLISH

EVERY DAY ENGLISH IDIOMS

DRITA SKILJA

 www.trafford.com
North America & international
toll-free: 1 888 232 4444 (USA & Canada)
fax: 812 355 4082

Dedication

To my beloved sons, Arber and Toni,
and to my adorable grandchildren,
Arba, Roan, and Sofia, who are
the love, joy, and hope in my life.

TABLE OF CONTENTS

PREFACE

1,001 Idioms to Master Your English is a useful collection for pre-intermediate to advanced English learners. It is written for those who want their English to be more natural and more fluent. It is written for those who want to feel more confident in understanding the real-life language, the language used in newspaper articles, magazines, literature, speeches, the workplace, school, radio, and television broadcasts, as well as in everyday informal conversation.

What is an idiom? An idiom is a group of words that has a completely different meaning from the meaning of each of its words taken separately. For example, an idiom such as "a piece of cake" is not used when there really is a piece of cake in front of you. Although you may know both words *piece* and *cake,* it is almost impossible to guess the meaning of this idiom unless you know that it is an idiom, which means something is *very easy to do.*

Idioms play an important part in understanding what is said. This book is designed to sort out the confusion caused by common idiomatic language. Without a good command of idiomatic expressions, students cannot feel completely comfortable and confident when they are in direct contact with colloquial English in an English-speaking country.

This collection contains twenty chapters covering 1,001 of the most common and useful idioms in English. To make the book more challenging and to get a lot of practice with such idioms, we have incorporated at the end of each unit a wide variety of exercises, ranging from matching idioms to gap-filling exercises.

—Drita Skilja

Here is a short dialogue that shows miscommunication between two friends because of a lack of knowledge of English idioms. Suzy is an English student, and Bill is a native speaker.

At a party

Bill: Hi Suzy, how do you like this Jack and Jill party?
Suzy: Oh, you must be wrong. Their names are Tom and Helen.
Bill: I know; they are my old buddies. But Jack and Jill means all men and women are invited. By the way, you look like a million bucks.
Suzy: No, I buy lottery tickets very often, but I have never won.
Bill: I know, but I mean you look gorgeous.
Suzy, Oh, thanks. I feel embarrassed. I didn't know. Would you like to dance?
Bill: Oh, I'm sorry, but I have two left feet.
Suzy: What's wrong with you? I can see your feet are all right.
Bill: Of course they are, but I mean I am a bad dancer.
Suzy: Oh, I see. By the way have you found a job yet?
Bill: No, it's so hard these days—catch-22.
Suzy: What? I don't get you. Who is catching you?
Bill: Well, it means they want experience, but how can I get experience when nobody hires me?! I'll be on cloud nine when I get my first job.
Suzy: Really? But there is not even a single cloud in the sky today.
Bill: No, Suzy, I mean I will be very happy. You need to learn idioms.
Suzy: I know; can you teach me some every day?
Bill: No problem, Bob's your uncle.
Suzy: I have no uncles. Who is Bob? Oh, I feel so embarrassed.

FOOD

A piece of cake—very easy to do

E.g., After studying for a long time, the test was a piece of cake.

The icing on the cake—the best part of something

E.g., Christmas last year was wonderful, but the icing on the cake was my sister's surprise visit.

That takes the cake—that's the worst; that's the limit; that's too much

E.g., Did you hear that James lost his wallet with $5,000 in it? That takes the cake, doesn't it?

A slice of the cake—a share of profits, benefits, etc.

E.g., When the three brothers' parents died, the eldest brother expected the biggest slice of the cake.

Can't have your cake and eat it too—it's impossible to have something both ways, if those two ways conflict. Once you have eaten your cake, you won't have it any more.

E.g., You want to lose weight but you must quit sugar. You can't have your cake and eat it, too.

Sell like hotcakes—sell fast

E.g., Danielle Steel's new book is selling like hotcakes.

A tough cookie—a stubborn, strong person

E.g., Don't try to make her change her mind. She is a tough cookie.

A smart cookie—intelligent person

E.g., My brother got into an Ivy League college; he has always been a smart cookie.

Get caught with your hand in the cookie jar—to be caught when doing something that is dishonest or illegal

E.g., Mike denied cheating on the test, but he got caught with his hand in the cookie jar.

That's the way the cookie crumbles—that is fate; that is the way things happen

E.g., You didn't win the lottery this time. That's the way the cookie crumbles

Life is just a bowl of cherries—life is wonderful

E.g., Ann loves her life right now. She always says, "Life is just a bowl of cherries."

The apple of one's eye—someone's favorite person

E.g., My granddaughter is the apple of my eye. I love being with her.

A rotten apple—undesirable character

E.g., Mike is the rotten apple in your group. You should be careful of him.

In apple-pie order—neat and orderly; arranged

E.g., When mother went home, she found everything in apple-pie order. Her children had put all their toys away.

Upset the apple cart—cause big problems

E.g., Don't tell dad I drove his car last night. You'll upset the apple cart.

The apple doesn't fall far from the tree—children are like their parents

E.g., Tony is good at fixing things, just like his dad. The apple doesn't fall far from the tree.

Big Apple—New York City
E.g., They had a great vacation in the Big Apple.

Your salad days—a time when you were young and inexperienced
E.g., When we get together with school friends, we talk about our salad days.

Bring home the bacon—earn enough to support the family
E.g., Amy is a single mom, and she works long hours to bring home the bacon.

Save your bacon—save you from risk
E.g., My son's quick idea to solve my problem saved my bacon.

Put all your eggs in one basket—invest everything in only one plan
E.g., He put all his eggs in one basket, and when his business failed, he was in trouble.

Walk on eggshells—acting very carefully
E.g., It seems like she is walking on eggshells. She doesn't want to make mistakes.

You can't make an omelet without breaking eggs—it's impossible to achieve something good without having unpleasant effects
E.g., If you want to pass the exams, you need to study much harder. You can't make an omelet without breaking eggs.

Butterfingers—a very clumsy person
E.g., my friend is so clumsy and always dropping things. She is a real butterfingers.

Bread and butter—the main source of profit
E.g., He sells variety of things, but computers are his bread and butter.

Break bread—share a meal with other people
E.g., We used to break bread when we were in the dorm.

Be toast—be destroyed; likely to be in trouble
E.g., If I don't submit my test by midnight, I am toast.

Cast one's bread upon the waters—do well with little or no prospect of reward
E.g., Before he retired, the manager gave everyone a raise. He cast his bread upon the waters.

Know on which side your bread is buttered—know what to do for your own advantage
E.g., Sam always has good relationships with his managers. He knows on which side his bread is buttered.

Half a loaf is better than none—having part of something is better than having nothing
E.g., She accepted her part-time job—half a loaf is better than nothing.

Cheesy—not cool; not trendy
E.g., No one liked her cheesy love song. It was so outdated.

Cup of tea—favorite activity; the best choice of entertainment
E.g., I love reading; it is my cup of tea.

A storm in the teacup—a lot of fuss about something which proves to be unimportant
E.g., The news made a big fuss about the hurricane, but it turned out to be only a storm in the teacup.

Cook your goose—ruin oneself; to be in trouble
> *E.g., If you borrow too much money for your business and do poorly, you will cook your goose.*

Couch potato—someone who watches a lot of TV
> *E.g., Their son is just a couch potato; he sits in front of TV for hours.*

Small potatoes—unimportant things
> *E.g., Don't worry about your car scratches; they are small potatoes.*

A hot potato—a topic that is considered dangerous
> *E.g., Talking about religion used to be a hot potato; it isn't a good thing to discuss.*

Drop someone like a hot potato—leave someone quickly
> *E.g., When she found out he was not rich, she dropped him like a hot potato.*

Cry in your beer—regret not having done something
> *E.g., Study hard and get your diploma, or someday you'll be crying in your beer because it didn't happen.*

Cry over spilt milk—waste time worrying about something that you cannot change
> *E.g., my friend was mad she broke her crystal vase, and I said, "Don't cry over spilt milk."*

Go bananas—become very excited and act wildly
> *E.g., Mary went bananas when she passed the exams.*

Be nuts—be crazy or insane; be out of one's mind
> *E.g., John must be nuts to pay so much for a used car.*

Everything from soup to nuts—from start to finish

E.g., Lisa told us everything about her trip to Mexico from soup to nuts.

A hard nut to crack—a difficult person or thing to deal with

E.g., be careful with the new boss; he is a hard nut to crack.

Peanuts—very cheap

E.g., I waited for this dress to go on sale, and I bought it for peanuts.

Drives me nuts—makes you crazy

E.g., the annoying noise of the boys on the bus drives me nuts.

In a nutshell—briefly; very quickly

E.g., let me tell you in a nutshell about my trip plans; it won't take long.

The cream of the crop—the best part of the group

E.g., only the cream of the crop will be invited to the interview

A lemon—something that does not work, usually an electrical or mechanical item

E.g., the new TV is a lemon, and I am going to take it back to the store.

A peach—a very nice, caring person

E.g., Mary is such a peach; she spent Saturday helping me cook the food for the party.

Like two peas in a pod—similar in many ways

E.g., my twin sister and I are like two peas in a pod; we love all the same things.

Through the grapevine—hear about something from other
people, not from the person who said it
*E.g., I heard through the grapevine that our company
manager will quit.*

Sour grapes—negative because you can't have something
*E.g., she couldn't afford buying that fur coat. She said she
just didn't like the color, but it's just sour grapes.*

The fruit of something—the good result of an activity
E.g., this book is the fruit of my hard work.

Spill the beans—tell a secret
*E.g., I won't trust her with my plan because she'll spill the
beans.*

Full of beans—very active or lively
*E.g., look at those boys running around; they are full of
beans.*

In a pickle—in trouble; in a difficult situation
E.g., I'll be in a pickle if my car runs out of gas.

Land someone in hot water—get someone in trouble
*E.g., he is not afraid to criticize his boss, but this often lands
him in hot water.*

Water under the bridge—something forgotten about
*E.g., "Aren't you angry with him that he dumped you?" I
asked.*
*"No, that was a long time ago. It's all water under the
bridge," she said.*

Hold water—when something is not strong, sound, or logical
E.g., his excuses about coming to school late don't hold water.

Throw cold water on a plan—to discourage a plan

E.g., her parents always throw cold water on her plans, and she changes her mind.

A real turkey—something that is a failure or does not work

E.g., her new movie is a real turkey; no one went to see it.

Cut the mustard—do the job properly

E.g., Sam should retire; he is too old to cut the mustard.

Drink like a fish—drink a lot, especially liquor

E.g., when Bob visits us, we buy a lot of beer because he drinks like a fish.

Hit the bottle—to get drunk

E.g., when they broke up, Michael hit the bottle in order to forget her.

Drive me nuts—cause one to feel crazy

E.g., the loud noise from the children is driving me nuts.

Eat humble pie—admit that you didn't do well

E.g., he had to face the facts and eat humble pie when he was not reelected.

A good egg—a good, reliable person

E.g., our new teacher seems like a good egg; this will be a good school year.

Egg on one's face—embarrassment

E.g., our boss promised to do a lot but ended up with egg on his face. He forgot about his promises.

Goose egg—zero; no score

E.g., they got five goals, and we got the goose egg.

Nest egg—money saved for retirement

E.g., they had saved money all their life and had a nest egg when they retired.

Not for all the tea in China—never, not even if you gave me everything

E.g., I wouldn't go back there to work—not for all the tea in China.

Rub salt in the wound—make the situation worse

E.g., do not criticize her in front of her friends. You are rubbing salt in the wound.

One man's meat is another man's poison—one person's preference may be disliked by another person

E.g., Cathy likes her fish soup, but I think it's horrible—one man's meat is another man's poison.

Bite off more than you can chew—try to do something that is too difficult

E.g., be sure that you don't bite off more than you can chew before you take on this difficult task.

Variety is the spice of life—it's good to try to do different things

E.g., we went to different places on our vacation to Cuba, feeling that variety is the spice of life.

The rest is gravy—the rest of the money is profit

E.g., After I pay expenses, the rest is gravy.

Too many cooks spoil the broth—a job will be mismanaged if too many people try to do it at once

E.g., my mom and dad were both making dinner for us when they figured out that they had both put salt in the soup—too many cooks spoil the broth.

A land flowing with milk and honey—a place where life is enjoyable

E.g., I don't think that this country is a land flowing with milk and honey; there is much poverty and hardship here.

Exercises

(1) Match the idioms with the definitions.

1.	the cream of the crop	a.	sell fast
2.	a lemon	b.	time when you were young and inexperienced
3.	a peach		
4.	break bread	c.	the best part of something
5.	icing on the cake		
6.	like hotcakes	d.	be careful
7.	your salad days	e.	very nice and caring person
8.	peanuts		
9.	walk on eggshells	f.	very cheap
10.	pie in the sky	g.	something that does no work
		h.	the best part of the group
		i.	share a meal with other people
		j.	unrealistic

(2) Finish these idioms with one of the following words:

nut, gravy, egg, cake, potato, bananas, bacon, fish, bread, butter, cookie, apple, beer, grape wine, pie, coffee

1. a smart _____
2. a rotten _____
3. can't have your _____ and eat it too
4. go _____
5. save your _____
6. a hard _____ to crack
7. bigger _____ to fry
8. cast one's_____ upon the waters

9.   _____ fingers
10. couch _____

(3) Is the speaker happy or unhappy when he/she:

   a.   buys something that is a lemon
   b.   has a friend that is a peach
   c.   buys something for peanuts
   d.   is in a pickle
   e.   cries in a beer
   f.   is in a stew
   g.   hits the bottle
   h.   lands someone in hot water

(4) Fill in the blanks with one of the following: under, with, upon, in, on, through.

   a.   _____ apple-pie order
   b.   pie _____ the sky
   c.   put all eggs _____ one basket
   d.   walk _____ eggshells
   e.   the icing _____ the cake
   f.   cast one's bread _____ the waters
   g.   _____ the grapevine
   h.   cry _____ your beer
   i.   egg _____ one's face
   j.   water _____ the bridge

(5) Complete the sentences so that they are true for you.

   a.   I had to eat humble pie when _____
   b.   _____ is a piece of cake for me.
   c.   _____ is the apple of my eye.
   d.   _____ is a pie in the sky.
   e.   _____ saved my bacon when _____
   f.   _____ is my cup of tea.

g. Talking about _____ is a hot potato.
h. I went bananas when _____
i. I was in a pickle when _____
j. I heard through the grapevine that _____

(6) **Find someone who:**

    a. cuts the mustard
    b. drinks like a fish
    c. is a smart cookie
    d. is a couch potato
    e. brings home the bacon
    f. has put all his/her eggs in one basket
    g. breaks bread
    h. has butterfingers
    i. likes coffee talk
    j. is in a pickle

(7) **Pair/group work: create your own situations using some of the food idioms.**

BODY

Keep a cool head—be calm in a difficult situation
E.g., he always keeps a cool head in difficult situations.

Above someone's head—beyond someone's ability to understand
E.g., when she was a young student, she thought that math was above her head.

Clear one's head/mind—relax so that you can think clearly
E.g., after the argument with her mother, Diana went out because she needed some time to clear her head.

Bang/bit/hit/knock one's head against a brick wall—waste one's efforts by trying to do something impossible
E.g., trying to get his students to learn everything was like banging his head against the wall.

Go to someone's head---make drunk
E.g., I go very easy on wine because it quickly goes to my head.

Have one's head in the clouds—not act according to the reality; have no idea what's going on
E.g., in the staff meeting he was asked about the most urgent matters, but he had his head above the clouds and didn't realize he was supposed to respond.

To be head and shoulders above—be much better than others
E.g., the best student in math, Tom is head and shoulders above everybody in the class.

Heads will roll—certain people will be punished for a big mistake they made
E.g., though he is still powerful, heads will roll, and he will have to make up for his mistake.

Hit the nail on the head—what was said is exactly right

E.g., *when the president called on the political parties to be more cooperative with each other, he hit the nail on the head; cooperation was very much needed.*

Bury one's head in the sand—hide from signs of danger; try to avoid bad news

E.g., *stop burying your head in the sand, and acknowledge the statistics on smoking and cancer.*

Off the top of one's head—make a rough guess

E.g., *off the top of my head I can tell you approximately how many people are in the room.*

Cannot make heads or tails of something—unable to understand something

E.g., *I have to read this chapter again because I couldn't make heads or tails of it.*

Have a good head on one's shoulders—to be sensible and intelligent

E.g., *he is doing a good job because he has a good head on his shoulders.*

Go head to head with someone—argue or fight with someone

E.g., *Paul and his wife are always disagreeing and going head to head about how to raise their children.*

Keep one's head above water—try to survive financially

E.g., *I haven't got a full-time job yet, but we are trying to keep our heads above water.*

Be at the head of something—be responsible for something; be in charge of something

E.g., *you should talk to my boss; he is at the head of the company.*

To get through one's head—understand

> *E.g., my brother spent four hours helping me get the concept of electricity through my head.*

Laugh your head off—laugh a lot

> *E.g., I laughed my head off when I he told us those hilarious jokes.*

Get a swelled head—be conceited

> *E.g., now that she is famous, she'll be getting a swelled head.*

Put one's head in the lion's mouth—put oneself in a dangerous position

> *E.g., he put himself in the lion's mouth when he broke into his neighbor's house.*

Have rocks in the head—have no sense when making decisions

> *E.g., if he goes hiking in this snow, he's got rocks in his head.*

Peace of mind—free from worry

> *E.g., he bought life insurance to have peace of mind.*

Speak one's mind—express one's thoughts directly

> *E.g., I'm furious about Fred's behavior at work, and I intend to speak my mind to the manager*

Your mind is blank—cannot remember anything

> *E.g., my friend did not pass the exam because her mind was blank.*

Brain drain—emigration of intelligent people

> *E.g., many of the country's best professional people have moved away—what a brain drain!*

Brains—intelligence

> *E.g., Agnes is brilliant; she has more brains than anyone else I know.*

Beat the brain—try hard to think

> *E.g., Toni was beating the brain, and finally he solved the math problem.*

Let one's hair down—enjoy oneself; start to relax, especially after working hard

> *E.g., the party gave us the chance to really let our hair down and relax.*

Get in someone's hair—annoy someone, especially by being continually present

> *E.g., she finds her children are always around and get in her hair during their school holidays.*

Keep your hair on—remain calm; do not get annoyed

> *E.g., I tried to keep my hair on when I heard that my car had been stolen.*

Make someone's hair stand on end—frighten someone

> *E.g., ghost stories make my hair stand on end.*

Pull one's hair out—be very anxious about something

> *E.g., she pulled her hair out waiting to see if her daughter had passed the exam.*

Fair-haired boy—favorite man

> *E.g., they all think that Robert is the fair-haired boy in this class; everyone loves him.*

Face to face—in person

> *E.g., the best way to criticize someone is when you are face to face.*

Have a long face—sad, dissatisfied

E.g., Mira has a long face because she did not get the job she applied for.

Fall flat on one's face—be completely unsuccessful

E.g., if our business doesn't work, we could fall flat on our face.

One's eyes are bigger than one's stomach—someone takes more food than they can eat

E.g., You won't be able to eat all that food. Your eyes are bigger than your stomach right now.

See eye to eye with someone—totally agree with someone

E.g., the two of them saw eye to eye and decided to buy the house.

In your mind's eye—in your imagination or memory

E.g., in my mind's eye my sons will always be little boys.

Have eyes in the back of one's head—seem to be able to sense what is going on outside one's vision

E.g., my teacher seems to have eyes in the back of his head when he yells at us without turning around from the chalkboard.

To pull the wool over someone's eyes—lie to someone so they don't see the truth

E.g., She always pulled the wool over her parents' eyes when they asked her why she kept getting home so late.

In the public eye—well known; in the news

E.g., Madonna has been in the public eye for years.

Keep one's eyes peeled—watch carefully

E.g., keep your eyes peeled for snakes when you are in the woods.

Cry one's eyes out—cry very hard
> *E.g., she cried her eyes out when she heard the news about her friend's death.*

To my eye—in one's opinion
> *E.g., to my eye, Sid's paintings are just beautiful.*

Roll one's eyes—express boredom or disapproval
> *E.g., when she told us about her daughter's grades, we all rolled our eyes because we had heard it many times before.*

Give one's eye teeth—give a lot; pay a lot to get something
> *E.g., she'd give her eye teeth to have her baby back.*

Up to the eyes—very busy
> *E.g., I can't go to the party tonight because I am up to the eyes in work.*

Catch one's eye—notice someone
> *E.g., let's ask the waiter for another bottle. Try to catch his eye.*

Cause one's eyebrows to raise—shock people; surprise and dismay people
> *E.g., he started singing as he was walking down the street and caused eyebrows to raise.*

Raise one's eyebrows—show surprise and disapproval
> *E.g., everybody raised their eyebrows at the president's insensitive comments.*

To make someone's mouth water—when a food is mentioned mention, you crave it/want it at that moment
> *E.g., the roasted turkey placed in the middle of the table made everybody's mouth water.*

To have a big mouth—talk too much and keep no secrets
E.g., do not trust her; she has a big mouth.

Down in the mouth—low in spirits
E.g., she is always down in the mouth when her friends go out and her parents do not allow her to go.

A bad taste in the mouth—a feeling that something is unfair or false
E.g., she left the meeting unhappy and with a bad taste in her mouth.

Born with a silver spoon in the mouth—having always had everything one wants
E.g., her brother has always been lucky; he must have been born with a silver spoon in his mouth.

Don't look a gift horse in the mouth—not be critical for something given as a gift
E.g., I didn't actually like my mother's birthday gift, but I said nothing to her. It's not nice to look a gift horse in the mouth.

Motor mouth—one who talks fast but says very little
E.g., listen to that motor mouth. No one is able to understand her.

Have a sweet tooth—like to eat sweet foods
E.g., he knows I have a sweet tooth, so he bought me a box of chocolates.

Long in the tooth—getting old
E.g., I can't run fast as I used to. I think I am getting long in the tooth.

Kick in the teeth—unfair remark

E.g., Not giving her a promotion after she had worked so hard, was a real kick in the teeth.

Grit your teeth—be determined to continue in a difficult, unpleasant situation

E.g., I gritted my teeth and studied hard to improve my grades.

To cut teeth—for a baby to grow teeth

E.g., the baby is so cranky because he is cutting teeth.

Lie through one's teeth—tell lies without any shame

E.g., after they divorced, we all said she had lied through her teeth about their perfect relationship.

Cut one's teeth on something—earn or gain experience for something

E.g., as a boy he cut his teeth on the waters of the river near his village. He is no newcomer to swimming.

To examine something with a fine-tooth comb—examine very carefully

E.g., we examined the records with a fine-tooth comb, looking at every aspect.

Fed up to the back teeth with something—extremely bored or dissatisfied with something

E.g., she was fed up to the back teeth with her long, boring cottage vacations.

By the skin of one's teeth—just managing to do something; nearly failing

E.g., I passed the exam by the skin of my teeth.

To talk tongue in cheek—say something as a joke, even if it seems serious
E.g., do not take what he said seriously; it was tongue in cheek.

Loosen somebody's tongue—make somebody talk a lot
E.g., the wine had certainly loosened her tongue.

Bite your tongue—hold your tongue to stop yourself from saying something unwise
E.g., I wanted to argue, but I had to bite my tongue in order to avoid conflict.

Slip of the tongue—a small mistake made while speaking; a mistake that is humorous or embarrassing
E.g., mispronouncing the word was only a slip of the tongue that made everybody laugh.

Tongue-tied—unable to say a word because one is feeling shy or nervous
E.g., the very first day they met, he was tongue-tied.

Cannot find one's tongue—unable to speak because of shock
E.g., he was so shocked that he could not find his tongue.

On the tip of one's tongue—not quite able to be remembered
E.g., I can't think of his name; it is on the tip of my tongue.

A sharp tongue—a tendency to reply sharply or sarcastically
E.g., Fred doesn't get along with his mother in law. He says she really has a sharp tongue.

Button your lips—don't let the secret out
E.g., don't tell anyone about this—button your lips.

My lips are sealed—keep a secret

E.g., don't worry—I will not tell anyone what you told me. My lips are sealed.

Keep a stiff upper lip—hide one's emotions

E.g., I could not keep a stiff upper lip, and I shared my feelings with her.

Read my lips—mean exactly what is said

E.g., read my lips: if you don't come to work on time, I'll fire you.

Jaw drops—be greatly surprised

E.g., my jaw dropped when my husband gave me a diamond ring I was not expecting.

Breathe down someone's neck—watch someone closely

E.g., I can't work here anymore with my boss hovering and breathing down my neck.

A pain in the neck—something or someone that annoys or bothers you

E.g., waiting for the bus in the rain is a pain in the neck.

To be up to one's neck—very busy

E.g., you seem to be up to your neck in work. I'll come back tomorrow.

To break one's neck on a job—try too hard

E.g., he was working very hard and breaking his neck on the new job.

To stick one's neck out—act despite the risk of danger or trouble

E.g., Vera is the kind of person who is willing to stick her neck out to help a friend in trouble.

Get it in the neck—receive criticism or punishment
> *E.g., Bill got it in the neck for being late.*

Risk one's neck—do something that could have dangerous consequences
> *E.g., my boss hates to spend money, but I risked my neck anyway and asked for a raise.*

Have a lump in one's throat—have a feeling in one's throat as if one were going to cry
> *E.g., when they play the national anthem, I get a lump in my throat.*

Cut one's own throat—hurt oneself
> *E.g., by speeding you will cut your own throat.*

Up to one's ears—deeply
> *E.g., she is up to her ears in debt.*

Lend me your ear—listen to me
> *E.g., could you lend me an ear for a minute so that I can tell you something?*

My ears are burning—feeling like someone is talking about you
> *E.g., my ears are burning; I think my parents are upset with me being late tonight.*

Shoulder to shoulder—work cooperatively
> *E.g., he was working shoulder to shoulder with his partners and succeeded in the end.*

Give someone the cold shoulder—deliberately ignore someone
> *E.g., After she was promoted as the manager of the company, Cathy gave her friends the cold shoulder.*

Put your shoulder to the wheel—put a great deal of effort into a difficult task

E.g., to be successful in business you have to put your shoulder to the wheel.

A shoulder to cry—rely on someone who gives you emotional support when you are upset

E.g., he needed a shoulder to cry on when he broke up with his wife.

Have a chip on his shoulder—angry about something; ready to fight

E.g., He seems to have a chip on his shoulder today. I would rather avoid talking to him.

Rub elbows—associate with someone

E.g., Tom loved rubbing elbows with celebrities.

Shot in the arm—encouragement at a time when you need it

E.g., Hiring a dedicated manager like Greg, was a shot in the arm for our company.

Twist someone's arm—persuade someone

E.g., I guess I'll have another chocolate, since you are twisting my arm.

Lead someone by the nose—have complete control over somebody

E.g., Elena leads her husband by the nose; he always listens to her.

Pay through the nose—pay too much for a service or product

E.g., he bought a very cheap used car, but he paid it through the nose by fixing its engine.

Keep one's nose out— not interfere in someone else's business
E.g., let me have my privacy, and keep your nose out of my business.

Keep one's nose clean—keep away from illegal actions
E.g., he is trying to keep his nose clean by staying away from the gang.

Under one's nose—in plain view
E.g., the robbers robbed the bank under everybody's nose.

Cut off one's nose to spite one's face—take a chance that harms one's own interests
E.g., Arthur cheated in the exam because he wanted to get a good mark, but he failed. He cut off his nose to spite his face.

Turn up one's nose—treat someone with scorn
E.g., Lily always turns up her nose at guys who are not handsome.

Count noses—count people
E.g., let me count noses, and I'll tell you how many people there are in this room.

Nose out of joint—upset about what happened
E.g., his nose is out of joint because we didn't invite him to the party.

Keep your nose clean—avoid getting into trouble
E.g., he was trying to keep his nose clean and didn't join his friends when they decided to rob the bank.

As plain as the nose on your face—very obvious
E.g., you are not very happy here—that's as plain as the nose on your face.

Make someone's blood boil—make someone very angry
E.g., My friend makes my blood boil when she comes late and doesn't even apologize.

Make someone's blood run cold—cause someone to be very frightened
E.g., the scary ghost story made my blood run cold.

Get blood from stone—try for an impossible task
E.g., you'll get blood from stone before you get money from your miserly brother.

In one's blood—in one's character
E.g., Dora is a very good singer. Singing is in her blood.

In cold blood—cruelly and without feeling
E.g., he was murdered in cold blood.

Break one's heart—cause someone emotional pain
E.g., it just broke my heart when Tom ran away from home and I never saw him again.

After one's own heart—similar to oneself; the type one likes
E.g., He likes the same movies and music as me. He is a man after my own heart.

Do not have the heart—do not want to tell someone something hurtful
E.g., I did not have the heart to tell her the bad news.

Have one's heart in one's mouth/boots—very scared or worried
E.g., when he was telling us what had happened to him and how awful it was, I had my heart in my mouth.

A change of heart—s changed opinion
> *E.g., there was a time when I had liked him, but as time went on, I had a change of heart.*

In one's heart of hearts—in reality; in one's most secret feelings
> *E.g., he told her that he loved her, but in his heart of hearts he knew it wasn't true.*

To take something to heart—feel the effect deeply
> *E.g., don't take his criticism to heart and let yourself get upset.*

Eat one's heart out—to suffer from jealousy or envy
> *E.g., Gabriella has been eating her heart out over that man since he left her.*

Lose one's heart to—fall in love with
> *E.g., Olivia has lost her heart to Ben and wants to marry him.*

Wear one's heart on one's sleeve—show one's true feelings openly instead of hiding them
> *E.g., everybody knows that Mary is in love with Tom. She is wearing her heart on her sleeve.*

Cross one's heart and hope to die—vow that you are telling the truth
> *E.g., what I just told you is really true—cross my heart and hope to die.*

A real heartthrob---a man who is so handsome that he makes your heart beat fast
> *E.g., Brad Pitt is a real heartthrob in Hollywood.*

Set one's heart on—want something badly and work hard to get it

E.g., my twin sister set her heart on becoming a dedicated doctor.

Have a heart of stone—be cruel and unkind

E.g., She wouldn't help her own children if they needed her. She has got a heart of stone.

Have a heart of gold—have a kind and generous character

E.g., Sarah helps me whenever she can. She has a heart of gold.

One's heart misses a beat—excited

E.g., my heart misses a beat whenever I see my boyfriend.

Have a heart-to-heart talk—have a sincere and intimate talk with someone

E.g., Good friends very often have heart-to-heart talks.

One's heart is in the right place—kind and generous

E.g., My boss is a bit annoying sometimes, but her heart is in the right place

Tug at your heart strings—cause you to feel a great deal of pity or sadness

E.g., Anna tugged at our heart strings when she told us her sad life story.

Pour out your heart—tell someone the most private thoughts and feelings

E.g., I learned a great deal about Tom when he poured out his heart to me about his divorce.

Cry one's heart/eyes out—cry a lot

E.g., Rita cried her heart out when her mother died.

Play the cards close to your chest/vest—keep it to yourself; be secretive or cautious

E.g., don't expect Michael to tell you much. He plays the cards close to his chest.

Can't stomach something—dislike something very much

E.g., I can't stomach violent movies.

Stab someone in the back—hurt someone when they trust you

E.g., Alex told everyone what you confided in him. He stubbed you in the back.

A pat on the back—a gesture of appreciation for doing something

E.g., when I told my parents that my sister went to the movie during school, they said I deserved a pat on the back for being honest.

Glad to see the back of someone—happy when a person leaves

E.g., my former manager bugged us all the time. We were glad to see the back of him.

Go behind someone's back—do something without telling someone

E.g., don't trust her. She seems friendly but she is always going behind someone's back.

Talk behind one's back—talk about someone when they are not there

E.g., if you want to criticize me, tell me to my face. If there's one thing I hate, it's people who talk behind my back.

Turn your back on someone—abandon someone

> E.g., I needed your help, but you turned your back on me and left.

Send a shiver down someone's spine—cause feelings of fear or horror

> E.g., The music of Mozart sends a shiver down my spine.

Keep one's fingers crossed—hope that something good will happen

> E.g., I am keeping my fingers crossed for you. I hope you get the job.

Get one's fingers burned—have a bad experience

> E.g., I tried to learn to ride a bicycle but I got my fingers burned. I will not try it again.

Work one's fingers to the bones—Work very hard for a long time, especially doing manual tasks

> E.g., for many years she worked her fingers to the bones at the factory.

Have sticky fingers—have a tendency to steal

> E.g., that little boy has sticky fingers when he goes to the candy store.

Point the finger—accuse someone

> E.g., the child pointed the finger to the man he had seen breaking into the house.

Have something at one's fingertips—have something ready at hand, able to get something very easily

> E.g., My students have their dictionaries at their finfertips.

Know like the back of your hand—know extremely well
> *E.g., after living in Toronto for a long time, she knows the city like the back of her hand.*

A firm hand—a person who will discipline people
> *E.g., Grade nine students may try to take advantage and need a teacher with a firm hand.*

Gets out of hand—uncontrollable
> *E.g., My neighbors' daughter has gotten out of hand. She has dropped out of school and parties until midnight.*

One's hands are tied—unable to act
> *E.g., I am in favor of a weekend party, but my hands are tied. I'll have to wait for my parents' decision.*

Hand in hand—holding each other's hand
> *E.g., the children are walking hand in hand next to each other.*

Have your hands full—very busy
> *E.g., when she gives birth to her third child, she will have her hands full.*

In the palm of your hand—under complete control
> *E.g., she has her boyfriend in the palm of her hand; he listens to all she says.*

Bite the hand that fed you—ungrateful to the one who helped you
> *E.g., everybody knows how helpful you have been to her, but she bit the hand that fed her.*

Wash one's hands of— refuse to be responsible
> *E.g., Jim washed his hands of his business because it was going down.*

Have the upper hand—have the power or advantage
E.g., when Tom negotiates with his business competitors, he tries hard to get the upper hand.

Get one's hands dirty—become involved with something illegal or shameful
E.g., I will not get my hands dirty by breaking the law.

Have clean hands—lacking guilt
E.g., the police took him in, but they let him go again because he had clean hands.

Give someone a hand—help someone out
E.g., that suitcase looks very heavy. Can I give you a hand?

Be an old hand at something—have a lot of experience in something
E.g., Sandra is an old hand at teaching English since she has done it for fifteen years.

A free hand—complete freedom to act
E.g., the teacher gave us a free hand in choosing the novels to read.

Sit on one's hands—do nothing
E.g., Tom was sitting on his hands instead of doing his homework.

Cement hands—unable to catch or hold something
E.g., Whenever she washes glasses, she breaks one or two of them. She has cement hands.

Try one's hands—try to do
E.g., Tom said he couldn't finish his homework, but his mother told him to try his hand at finishing it.

Oil someone's palm—bribe someone
> *E.g., there are rumors that Matthew got his promotion by oiling his manager's palm.*

Have an itchy palm—waiting to get a tip
> *E.g., All taxi drivers have itchy palms.*

Be under one's thumb—be strongly influenced by someone that controls you completely
> *E.g., she just turned twenty-five but was still under her father's thumb.*

Turn thumbs down—disagree strongly with an idea
> *E.g., Ruben turned thumbs down to the project, and he refuses to support it financially.*

All thumbs—clumsy or awkward
> *E.g., my neighbor is all thumbs. He can not fix anything.*

Thumb one's nose—make a gesture of contempt by putting the thumb to the nose
> *E.g., she thumbed her nose at her brother when he made fun of her.*

Shake a leg—hurry up
> *E.g., it's late—shake a leg or we'll miss the plane.*

With one's tail between one's legs—very ashamed,; embarrassed and humiliated because of defeat or a mistake
> *E.g., the defeated soldiers retreated with their tails between their legs.*

Break a leg—good luck (especially to actors)
> *E.g., before the interview we all said to her, "Break a leg."*

Cost an arm and a leg—very expensive
E.g., the new car cost me an arm and a leg.

Pull someone's leg—kid or trick someone
E.g., Lisa told us it was her birthday, but it wasn't true. She was pulling our leg.

Not have a leg to stand on—have no support for an argument or a case
E.g., his lawyer said he didn't have a leg to stand on, so he shouldn't sue the company.

The first leg—the first part of a trip
E.g., the first leg of our trip was better because the weather was wonderful.

Have one's feet on the ground—be firmly established
E.g., he is new in Canada, but soon he'll get his feet on the ground.

Put one's foot in one's mouth—say something that you embarrass yourself
E.g., When I told Bob that his girlfriend was beautiful, I put my foot in my mouth. She was his sister.

Get one's feet wet—have one's first experience of something; to begin something
E.g., young people can't wait to drive on their own and get their feet wet.

Have itchy feet—greatly want to go somewhere
E.g., I had itchy feet to visit my home country.

Put one's foot down—be firm
E.g., Fatima put her foot down and refused to meet the matchmaker.

Start off on the wrong foot—have an unsuccessful beginning
> *E.g., Tim's new business started on the wrong foot when he hired inexperienced cooks.*

Think on one's feet—think quickly
> *E.g., they asked me unexpected questions in the interview. I had to think on my feet.*

Stand on one's own feet—be independent
> *E.g., Elisabeth turned twenty-four and told her parents that it was time she stood on her own feet.*

Put one's best foot forward—try one's best
> *E.g., you have to put your best foot forward to get the job you like.*

Find your feet—learning what to do
> *E.g., Ana has only been at this job for a few weeks. She's just finding her feet.*

Dead on my feet—very tired or exhausted
> *E.g., after working for fourteen hours, I was dead on my feet.*

Get cold feet—lose the courage to do something that is planned
> *E.g., they got cold feet at the last minute and refused to sign the contract.*

Drag one's feet—work very slowly
> *E.g., they are supposed to finish painting the room by six, but obviously they are dragging their feet.*

Be under one's feet – you prevent someone from doing what they want to be doing
> E.g., I am cleaning the living room. Please stop being under my feet.

On one's toes—alert

E.g., I have to be on my toes if I want to succeed in my new job.

Cool one's heels—wait long for someone

E.g., I spent all day cooling my heels and waiting for her.

Out on a limb—put yourself in a risky situation

E.g., we all would go out on a limb to help our children if they asked us to.

Over my dead body—not allow something to happen

E.g., I told my mom, "All my friends are going to a midnight party tonight and I'm going with them."
She said, "Over my dead body you are."

Have a thick (thin) skin—be insensitive (sensitive) to criticism

E.g., Rita's daughter has a thick skin. She won't change her habit of coming home so late.

Get under someone's skin—get on someone's nerves; annoy or irritate someone

E.g., children who scream and shout get under my skin and drive me crazy.

In one's bones—have a deep-seated feeling

E.g., I knew in my bones this was going to happen.

A bag of bones—very thin

E.g., she has put on a lot of weight. I remember she was just a bag of bones.

Exercises

(1) Match the idioms with their definitions.

1.	lend me your ear	a.	work very slowly
2.	off the top of one's head	b.	in plain view
		c.	to fall in love with
3.	have a sweet tooth	d.	express boredom
4.	button your lips	e.	make a rough guess
5.	roll one's eyes	f.	love to eat sweets
6.	beat the brain	g.	don't let the secret out
7.	down in the mouth	h.	please, listen to me
8.	under one's nose	i.	try hard to think
9.	lose one's heart to	j.	in low spirits
10.	drag one's feet		

(2) Finish these idioms with one of the following words:

lip, head, hair, stomach, face, tooth, eyebrows, tongue, ears, shoulder

a. my _____ are burning
b. bite your _____
c. keep a stiff upper _____
d. let one's _____ down
e. cause _____ to raise
f. have a long _____
g. one's eyes are bigger than one's _____
h. long in the _____
i. give someone the cold _____
j. have one's _____ in the clouds

(3) Is the speaker happy or unhappy when:

a. he gets his fingers burned
b. someone breathes down his neck

c. he cannot make heads or tails of something
d. he has a long face
e. he sees eye to eye with his friends
f. he is up to the eyes in work
g. he was born with a silver spoon in his mouth
h. he is down in the mouth
i. he gets it in the neck
j. someone gives him the cold shoulder

(4) Fill in the blanks with the following:

in, above, on, down, under, with, over, off, out, at

a. to be head and shoulders _____ others
b. have one's head _____ the clouds
c. hit the nail _____ the head
d. _____ the top of one's head
e. be _____ the head of something
f. pull the wool _____ someone's eyes
g. cry one's eyes _____
h. breathe _____ one's neck
i. _____ open arms
j. _____ one's nose

(5) Complete the sentences so that they are true for you.

a. I was knocking my head against a brick wall when _____
b. I kept a cool head when _____
c. I promised to keep my lips sealed when _____
d. I was up to one's neck in work when _____
e. I spoke my mind to _____
f. I tried to keep my hair on when _____
g. I had a long face when _____
h. I usually see eye to eye with _____
i. I remember falling flat on my face when _____

j.   I cried my eyes out when _____

(6) Find someone who:

a.   is head and shoulders above the others
b.   has a sharp tongue
c.   is a pain in the neck
d.   has a big mouth
e.   is a motor mouth
f.   is getting long in the tooth
g.   has a sweet tooth
h.   was born with a silver spoon in their mouth
i.   has a chip on his/her shoulder
j.   wears her/his heart on her/his sleeve

(7) Pair/group work: create your own situations using some of the body idioms.

ANIMALS

A snake in the grass—a person who cannot be trusted
> *E.g., I am not telling her about my plans. She is just a snake in the grass.*

Be a chicken—afraid
> *E.g., Monica is a chicken because she never drives on the highway.*

Chicken feed—very little money
> *E.g., what she makes from her part-time job is chicken feed.*

Go to bed with chickens—go to bed very early
> *E.g., when I am tired, I go to bed with chickens.*

No spring chicken—not young and strong anymore
> *E.g., Jeff can't play soccer as he used to. He is no spring chicken anymore.*

A chicken in every pot—enough food for every one
> *E.g., No one will be hungry if there is a chicken in every pot.*

Don't count the chickens before they are hatched—don't make plans before you get the results
> *E.g., "I think we can be sure we're going to win the elections. Look at the polls," I said.*
> *"Anything can happen the last few days. Don't count the chickens before they are hatched," he replied.*

Talk turkey—talk openly, directly
> *E.g., we were talking around the problem for about thirty minutes before we finally decided to talk turkey.*

A real turkey—something that is a failure or does not work
> *E.g., Her new movie is a real turkey. It did not do well at the box office.*

Cold turkey—quit immediately
E.g., Jeff wants to quit smoking right now. He is going cold turkey.

Rule the roost—make all the decisions
E.g., Many years ago, husbands ruled the roost and wives had little say.

Work like a dog—work very hard
E.g., You have to work like a dog if you want to keep two jobs and go to college as well.

Let sleeping dogs lie—don't cause or make trouble if you don't have to
E.g., Don't interfere in their argument. Let sleeping dogs lie.

Every dog has its day—everyone will get a chance
E.g., you may be famous one day—every dog has its day.

Dogs are barking—one's feet are hurting
E.g., after shopping all day, my dogs are barking, and I need to sit down.

Gone to the dogs—in very poor condition
E.g., my garden has gone to the dogs; the flowers are all dying.

The barking dog never bites—threaten but not do much damage
E.g., Max yells but has no fear—the barking dog never bites.

Eat like a horse—eat a lot
E.g., after running for three hours, he went home and ate like a horse.

Hold your horses—slow down and be reasonable
E.g., don't get so mad; just hold your horses.

Get off the high horse—do not act like you are better than
  anyone else
  *E.g., no one likes our line manager. Someone should tell him
  to get off his high horse.*

Change horses in midstream—make major changes in an
  activity which has already begun
  *E.g., I have started to write a detective story. I can't change it
  to a love story. You can't change horses in midstream.*

**Lock the stable door after the horse has escaped/is
  stolen**—try to prevent a loss when it is too late
  *E. g., A burglar broke into my neighbor's house and stole
  valuable things, so the next day he installed an alarm system.
  However, it was too late. It was like locking the stable door
  after the horse had escaped.*

A dark horse—someone who is reserved about their
  feelings, abilities, or plans
  *E.g., Robert is a dark horse. I would never have thought he
  could play the guitar as well as he does.*

Straight from the horse's mouth—directly from the source
  *E.g., I got the news of Ben's engagement to Laura straight
  from the horse's mouth; Ben told me himself.*

Donkey work—uninteresting work
  E.g., Mary is bored, doing the donkey work in this company.

Donkey's years—for a very long time
  E.g., I haven't seen my cousin for donkey's years.

A copycat—a person who imitates other people by what
  they do
  *E.g., Helen always wears the same clothes as her friend Dora.
  She is such a copycat.*

There is more than one way to skin a cat—more than one way to do something

E.g., if you can't solve the problem that way, try another way. There is more than one way to skin the cat.

It's raining cats and dogs—raining heavily

E.g., it rained cats and dogs during out trip to the beach; so much for getting some sun.

Like a cat on a hot tin roof—very nervous or anxious

E.g., Catherine was like a cat on a hot tin roof waiting for her blood test results.

Put the cat among the pigeons—cause trouble, especially by doing or saying something that makes people unhappy or angry.

E.g., By telling us that we had to work on Saturday, the manager put the cat among the pigeons

A cat burglar –a burglar who enters a house by climbing a wall

E.g., I saw a cat burglar entering the house across the street and called the police.

Fat cat—a rich and powerful person that misuses his/her money or power

E.g., He is a fat cat who contributed a lot in the political campaign and got a high position in the Conservative Party.

Not enough room to swing a cat—very little space

E.g., we can't invite more than ten people to my party. There is not enough room to swing a cat in my house.

Curiosity killed the cat—it is dangerous to be too curious

E.g., Tom, I heard you got a divorce. Mind your own business, Laura, – curiosity killed the cat.

Cat's paw—a person used by another to do something hard or dangerous

E.g., young kids sometimes become the cat's paw of older kids who need their help.

An early bird—a person who gets out of bed early or is the first person to be somewhere

E.g., Matthew is an early bird. He arrives before everyone else in the classroom.

A little bird told me—told something from a secret source

E.g., Thanks, Dennis, for the lovely flowers. How did you know it is my birthday?
"A little bird told me, Dora.

Bird brain—stupid person

E.g., he won't be able to give you any advice; he is just a bird brain.

Birds of a feather flock together—people of the same type gather together

E.g., they very often go out together because they share the same hobbies and interests. They are birds of a feather flock together.

The early bird gets the worm—the early person will get the reward

E.g., the early people at the party got the best food—he early bird gets the worm.

Kill two birds with one stone—accomplish two things with one action

E.g., When Emma came to Toronto, she visited CN tower and met her friends too. She killed two birds with one stone.

A home bird—someone who spends most of their free time at home

E.g., my husband is a home bird; he likes to spend all weekend around the house.

Snow birds—people who go to warm places in the South during winter

E.g., My snowbird neighbors leave Maine and go to Florida every winter.

Like a bat out of hell—very fast

E.g., He had a fight with his boss and just left the office like a bat out of hell.

Go ape—become extremely angry

E.g., he went ape when his son came home at 2:00 a.m.

Crocodile tears—fake tears

E.g., everyone knew she shed crocodile tears at her husband's funeral. She had never loved him.

Smell a rat—think that something is wrong

E.g., the man tried to sell me a gold watch for only five dollars, but I smelled a rat.

A big fish – an important, powerful person in an organization or group of people

E.g., Mrs. Osborne is a big fish in our company.

Fishing for compliments—saying something that encourages another person to compliment you

E.g., Mary said, "I think I look fat in this dress." She was fishing for compliments, hoping John would say, "No you don't; you look great."

Feel like a fish out of water—feel out of place; uncomfortable in a situation
E.g., Tom felt like a fish out of water at his friend's party since didn't know anyone there.

Have other fish to fry—have more important things to do
E.g., I can't waste time on your question. I have other fish to fry.

Fish for something—try to get information
E.g., When the phone rang, someone was fishing for too much information, so I hang up.

Plenty more fish in the sea—there are other options/people
E.g., you are better off without him since he was so selfish. There are plenty more fish in the sea.

A cold fish—a cold person
E.g., I've never seen the manager smile or laugh. He is a cold fish.

Neither fish nor fowl—not recognizable
E.g., this idea is neither fish nor fowl. I can't tell what your point is.

A fine/pretty cattle of fish--- a difficult situation
E.g., That's a pretty kettle of fish. The bus is getting late and I will be late for the interview.

A whale of a time—a lot of fun
E.g., What a party! We had a whale of a time.

Like water off a duck's back—have no effect in changing one's feelings or opinion
E.g., all of their advice to their daughter was ignored. It was like water off a duck's back.

Get one's ducks in a row—put one's affairs in order

E.g., as soon as we get our ducks in order and feel comfortable with the situation, we'll leave.

To buy a pig in a poke—buy something without having seen it

E.g., He ordered a suit by mail but it was the wrong color. He bought a pig in a poke.

Pigheaded—stubborn; not take advice

E.g., The young girl never listens to her parents. She is so pigheaded.

Cast pearls before swine—give something good to someone who doesn't care about it

E.g., Giving advice to some young people is like casting pearls to the swine.

When pigs fly—something that will never happen

E.g., I asked, "Do you think you will ever win a lottery?" She said, "When pigs fly."

To pig out—eat too much

E.g., Tom and his roommates pig out on chips on the weekends.

Keep the wolf from the door—keep from starving

E.g., he doesn't make a lot of money, just enough to keep the wolf from the door.

Cry wolf—complain about something when really nothing is wrong

E.g., if you cry wolf too often, no one will come.

A lone wolf---a person who prefers to do things alone, without others' help

E.g., Bill is a lone wolf until he has two glasses of wine.

The wolf is at the door---- the threat of poverty is on us
  E.g., When I lost my job, the wolf was at the door.

A wolf in sheep's clothing—someone who seems to be friendly or harmless but is in fact dangerous or dishonest
  E.g., Don't trust Tom—he is a wolf in sheep's clothing.

Big frog in a small pond—an important person in a small environment
  E.g., our company is very small, but Tom, our manager, likes being a big frog in a small pond.

Black sheep—a member of the family or group who is a disgrace
  E.g., Ron is the black sheep of the family. He is always in trouble with the police.

Kill the fatted calf—prepare a big meal in someone's honor
  E.g., when Mira finished college, her parents killed the fatted calf and threw a great party.

A wild goose chase—a waste of time; a long chase without results
  E.g., The police were looking everywhere for the stolen money, but it was a wild goose chase.

Kill the goose that laid the golden egg—destruct the source of one's good fortune
  E.g., the manager fired the best employee. He killed the goose that laid the golden egg.

Have a cow—become very angry
  E.g., I expected dad to have a cow when I told him I had broken his car mirror.

Fly in the ointment—a small, unpleasant matter which spoils something
E.g., We had a good time at the beach, but the fly in the ointment was the rain the last three days.

Wouldn't hurt a fly—a person is very gentle and not likely to hurt anyone
E.g., I don't believe Fred did it. He wouldn't hurt a fly.

Be like a bear with a sore head—be rude to people because you are feeling bad tempered
E.g., Don't ask the manager for help today. He is like a bear with a sore head.

Social butterfly—someone who has many friends and attends many social engagements
E.g., Mary is such a social butterfly. She would never miss a party.

A bee in her bonnet—upset
E.g., the school principle looks kind of cranky, like she has a bee in her bonnet.

A bull in a china shop—a reckless person in a fragile situation
E.g., they didn't invite Tom to their tea party. They said he would be like a bull in a china shop because of his size amongst all of the antique teapots.

A red rag to a bull—something very likely to provoke a strong reaction
E.g., any mention of dating is like a red rag to a bull for her mother.

Bitten by the same bug—have the same interests

E.g., my friend and I were bitten by the same bug. We both loved to collect stamps.

Eat crow—accept an error

E.g., the minister had to eat crow and apologize in Parliament for his blunder.

Eager beaver—enthusiastic person

E.g., The volunteer in my English class is an eager beaver.

A white elephant—something expensive but not useful

E.g., The modern coffee machine my neighbor bought me is a white elephant. I have no place for it.

Exercises

(1) Match the following idioms with their meanings.

1.	like water off a duck's back	a.	put one's affairs in order
2.	like birds of a feather	b.	have more important things to do
3.	a snake in the grass	c.	slow down and be reasonable
4.	smell a rat		
5.	chicken feed	d.	the disgrace of the family
6.	have other fish to fry	e.	a person who cannot be trusted
7.	hold your horses	f.	think there may be something wrong
8.	fly in the ointment	g.	very little money
9.	black sheep of the family	h.	without any effect
10.	get one's ducks in a row	i.	a small, unpleasant matter
		j.	very similar

(2) Put the following idioms in the sentences below:

a. swing a cat
b. eat crow
c. keep the wolf from the door
d. get goose bumps
e. an early bird
f. a copy cat

1. Mary's little sister wants to look like her elder sister. She buys the same toys and clothes as Mary. She is _____.
2. Mira is always the first to arrive at school. She's _____.

3. When I listen to our folk music, I always _____.
4. We can't have a party in this room. It's so small. We can't _____.
5. She was caught red-handed stealing her friend's makeup. She had to _____ and apologize.
6. He couldn't find a part-time job just to _____.

(3) Is the speaker happy or unhappy when:

1. he works like a dog
2. he has a donkey work
3. he is an early bird
4. he feels like a fish out of water
5. he buys a pig in a poke
6. he has a bee in her bonnet
7. it is raining cats and dogs
8. he is like a bear with a sore head

(4) Fill in the blanks with the following:

from, to, off, in, with, among

a. a snake _____ the grass
b. gone _____ the dogs
c. get _____ the high horse
d. put the cat _____ the pigeons
e. straight _____ the horse's mouth
f. plenty of fish _____ the sea
g. like water _____ a duck's back
h. a wolf _____ sheep's clothing

(5) Complete the sentences so that they are true for you.

a. I go to bed with chickens when _____.
b. I am a chicken when _____.

c. I had a bee in my bonnet when _____.
d. I was like a cat on a hot tin roof when _____.
e. I get goose bumps when _____.
f. It was a wild goose chase when _____.
g. I had to work like a dog when _____.

(6) Find someone who:

a. is no spring chicken
b. works like a dog
c. wouldn't hurt a fly
d. is a social butterfly
e. is like a bear with a sore head
f. goes to bed with chickens
g. eats like a horse

(7) Pair/group work: create your own situations using some of the animal idioms.

MONEY

Hit the jackpot—be very lucky

E.g., a couple from North York hit the jackpot last week and won two million dollars.

Look like a million dollars—look gorgeous

E.g., My friend, Nancy looked like a million dollars in that blue dress.

Feel like a million dollars—feel very healthy and happy

E.g., when Isabella returned from a relaxing, long holiday, she felt like a million dollars.

Million-dollar question—very important but difficult question

E.g., the million-dollar question is whether we should tell our friend that her husband is cheating on her or not.

Phony as a three-dollar bill—not genuine

E.g., I do not believe her excuses. They are as phony as a three-dollar bill.

Stretch the dollar—use the money carefully

E.g., If you only have a part-time job, you must stretch the dollar.

Top dollar--- the highest price

E.g., He paid top dollar to buy that lake view penthouse.

Save for a rainy day—save for future needs

E.g., I could manage to get by when I lost my job because I had saved some money for a rainy day.

Money talks—money gives power and influence

E.g., When we want good service, money talks.

Money burns a hole in someone's pocket—someone
spends money as soon as it is received/earned
*E.g., Sally can't seem to save anything. Money burns a hole
in her pocket.*

Have money to burn—have much money, usually more
than is needed
E.g., her uncle is so rich that he has money to burn.

Spend money like water—spend money without thinking
*E.g., My friend used to spend money like water when she
had a full time job, but when she lost her job, she realized she
should had saved some money for a rainy day.*

See the color of someone's money—verify
*E.g., before I sign this business contract, I want to see the
color of your money.*

Put your money where your mouth is—do something
rather than just talk about it
*E.g., You keep talking about your business plans— put your
money where your mouth is.*

Pin money—spending money; small amounts of money
that you spend for fun
*E.g., Her daughter makes some pin money by babysitting her
neighbor's little daughter every weekend.*

Put your money where your mouth is--- act and follow up
on what you say with action
*E.g., If the politicians are talking about improving the
people's lives, they should put their money where there
mouth is.*

Money is no object—it doesn't matter how much something costs

E.g., please, show me your finest car. Money is no object.

Hush money—money given to someone so that they will keep quiet

E.g., she was given hush money not to talk to the police about what she had seen.

Money doesn't grow on trees—money should be valued because may be limited

E.g., I can't afford to buy that brand new car. Money doesn't grow on trees.

More money than brains—someone has a lot of money but not the intelligence to use it well

E.g., he had a lot of money, but he never used it correctly. He had more money than brains.

Spend money like there is no tomorrow—spend money foolishly, not saving for the future

E.g., My friend is a shopaholic and she spends money like there is no tomorrow.

(not)have two cents to rub together--- to not have much money

E.g., When I got back from my vacations, I was broke and I did not have two cents to rub together.

A penny for your thoughts—tell me what you are thinking about

E.g., what are you thinking about? A penny for your thoughts.

Ten a penny—very common and easy to get

E.g., I split up with my boyfriend, but I never liked him. Men like him are ten a penny.

Pinch pennies—stingy

> *E.g., My friend is so stingy. She pinches pennies even now that she has a full time job.*

A dime a dozen—very cheap and common

> *E.g., I didn't buy anything in that store. Everything was a dime a dozen.*

Charity begins at home—be kind to one's own family before trying to help others

> *E.g., My neighbor spends*

Pick up the tab—pay for the cost of something, often a meal

> *E.g., we get to go to the annual Christmas party for free since our company picks up the tab.*

Cut corners—save money by economizing

> *E.g., they had to save and cut corners when he lost his job.*

It's a steal—very cheap

> *E.g., my new suit was a steal; I only paid fifty dollars.*

Live from hand to mouth—live on a day-to-day basis

> *E.g., when her husband had only a part-time job, they lived from hand to mouth.*

A cash cow—a good investment

> *E.g., Renting one of the rooms in his house is a real cash cow.*

Be broke—have no money

> *E.g., do you have an extra ten dollars that you can lend me? I am completely broke.*

Be well off—rich; having plenty of money

> *E.g., after he won the lottery, he was well off.*

From rags to riches—from poor to wealthy

E.g., her uncle won four million dollars and went from rags to riches.

Laugh all the way to the bank—make a lot of money without trying very hard

E.g., he laughed all the way to the bank from doing so well at his wholesale business.

Make a killing—make a lot of money

E.g., Robert made a killing when his business became successful.

Exercises

(1) Match the idioms with their definitions.

1.	foot the bill	a.	from poor to wealthy
2.	hit the jackpot	b.	very cheap
3.	it's a steal	c.	feel very healthy
4.	money talks	d.	be stingy
5.	be broke	e.	no money, no service
6.	well off	f.	be very lucky
7.	ten a penny	g.	pay the cost, especially
8.	feel like a million		a meal
	dollars	h.	penniless
9.	pinch pennies	i.	rich
10.	from rags to riches	j.	very common and easy
			to get

(2) Finish these idioms with the following words:

dollar, penny, corners, bill, dime, cash, pennies, water, money, tab

1. pinch _____
2. a _____ a dozen
3. a _____ cow
4. to have _____ to burn
5. a _____ saved is a _____ earned
6. spend money like _____
7. pick up the _____
8. stretch the _____
9. to cut _____

(3) Is the speaker feeling happy or unhappy when he/she:

1. buys something that is not worth a dime
2. feels like a million dollars

3. hits the jackpot
4. buys something that is a steal
5. is broke
6. has money to burn

(4) Fill in the blanks with the following:

up, on, at, off, in, for, from, by, to

1. save money _____ a rainy day
2. to live _____ hand to mouth
3. money burns a hole _____ his pocket
4. be well _____
5. a penny _____ your thoughts
6. money doesn't grow _____ trees
7. charity begins _____ home
8. to get _____
9. _____ the other side of the coin

(5) Complete the sentences so that they are true.

1. I felt like a million dollars when _____.
2. _____ cost me a fortune
3. _____ was a steal.
4. I was broke when _____.
5. Everyone knows that _____ has money to burn.
6. _____ I bought last year was not worth a dime.
7. _____ spends money like there is no tomorrow.
8. I had to cut corners when _____.
9. I picked up the tab when _____.
10. I tried to get by when _____.

(6) Find someone who:

1. has hit the jackpot
2. looks like a million dollars
3. saves money for a rainy day
4. has bought something that was not worth a dime
5. lives from hand to mouth
6. spends money like water
7. stretches the dollar
8. earns pin money
9. is broke
10. has old money

(7) Pair/group work: create your own situations using some of the money idioms.

COMPARISONS

As hungry as a horse/bear—very hungry
> *E.g., the children are as hungry as a bear. Let's stop for lunch right now.*

As healthy as a horse—very healthy
> *E.g., after she recovered, she felt as healthy as a horse.*

As sick as a dog—very sick
> *E.g., Alice is as sick as a dog and won't be going to school.*

As sharp as a tack—quick in understanding
> *E.g., my father is over seventy-five, but he's as sharp as a tack.*

Nutty as a fruitcake—funny, strange, or silly
> *E.g., After what he said to the manager, everyone thought Tim is as nutty as a fruitcake.*

Quick like a bunny—very quick
> *E.g., Mom told her son to run and get to bed quick like a bunny.*

White as a sheet—look pale
> *E.g., after she told me the scary story of what had happened to her, I was as white as a sheet.*

In a cold sweat—extremely frightened
> *E.g., when I saw the horrific accident, I broke out in a cold sweat.*

As hard as nails—tough; having no feelings
> *E.g., the lawyer was as hard as nails. He showed no pity.*

As easy as duck soup—very easy to do
> *E.g., finding your way to the shopping center is as easy as duck soup.*

As comfortable as an old shoe—very comfortable
E.g., this old house is fine. It's as comfortable as an old shoe.

As different as night and day—completely different
E.g., Although Bill and Bob are twins, they are as different as night and day.

As proud as a peacock—very proud and pleased with someone or something
E.g., he is as proud as a peacock of his daughter. She just graduated from medical school.

As cool as a cucumber—very calm and relaxed
E.g., he was as cool as a cucumber during the emergency.

As dead as a doornail—completely dead; no sign of life
E.g., the batteries are as dead as a doornail. No wonder this radio doesn't work.

As flat as a pancake—very flat
E.g., I can't drive my car. One tire is as flat as a pancake.

As free as a bird—carefree; completely free
E.g., in the summer I feel as free as a bird.

As easy as pie—very simple; very easy to do
E.g., I thought making this kind of cake was very difficult, but it was as easy as pie.

As poor as a church mouse—have very little money
E.g., how will he find the money to buy a car? He is as poor as a church mouse.

As busy as a hibernating bear—not busy at all
> *E.g., I asked my friend to help me with my paper work because she was as busy as a hibernating bear. She had been playing computer games for hours.*

As busy as a beaver—very busy, working steadily
> *E.g., Toni has been as busy as a beaver with his homework since he started high school.*

As clean as a whistle—clean; without any dirt
> *E.g., Mother cleaned up the dishes and made them as clean as a whistle.*

As useless as a fifth wheel—not needed; useless
> *E.g., I promised to help with the cooking before the party, but when I got there everything was done and I felt as useless as a fifth wheel.*

As happy as a lark/box of birds—very happy, joyful
> *E.g., the kids were as happy as a lark when they went to their grandparents.*

As clear as a bell—easy to hear or understand
> *E.g., we could understand everything he said. It was as clear as a bell.*

As drunk as a skunk—very drunk
> *E.g., at the reunion, he had a lot of wine and got drunk as a skunk.*

As scarce as hen's teeth—rare
> *E.g., doctors in remote villages are as scarce as hen's teeth.*

As clear as mud—not clear
> *E.g., our math teacher tried to explain the problem, but it was as clear as mud. We understood nothing.*

As mad as a hatter—strange or funny
E.g., we all thought you were mad as a hatter when we saw you singing alone on the road.

As high as the sky—very high
E.g., our pet bird flew as high as the sky.

As innocent as a lamb—1.naïve 2. innocent
E.g., Though he got married, he is still as innocent as a lamb.
E.g. The police arrested him, but they released him in two hours as he was as innocent as a lamb.

As light as a feather—very light; of little weight
E.g., stop dieting—you are as light as a feather.

As plain as day—clear and understandable
E.g., the lecture was as plain as day and I didn't have to think much.

As pretty as a picture—very pretty
E.g., their house was as pretty as a picture.

As quick as a wink—very quickly
E.g., I thought I would finish this book as quick as a wink, but it took me almost eight months.

As regular as clockwork—very regularly
E.g., She comes to the class every day, as regular as clockwork.

As sly as a fox—not to be trusted
E.g., how can she trust Michael? Everyone knows he is as sly as a fox.

Sick as a parrot—annoyed because of missing a great opportunity
> *E.g., I was sick as parrot when I found out I had torn my lottery ticket by mistake.*

As strong as an ox—very strong
> *E.g., Now that she is recovered from her illness, she is as strong as an ox.*

As solid as a rock— very strong building
> *E.g., the house seems sturdy and as solid as a rock.*

Safe as houses—very safe
> *E.g., "Aren't you worried about your job?" I asked.*
> *"No, I am a banker. My job is as safe as houses," he said.*

As stubborn as a mule—very stubborn
> *E.g., they are always fighting because she is as stubborn as a mule.*

As weak as a kitten—weak and sick
> *E.g., this boy is weak as a kitten because he doesn't eat well.*

As white as snow—very white
> *E.g., this little cat's fur is as white as snow.*

As slow as a snail—very slowly
> *E.g., she had worked hard all day and walked home as slow as a snail.*

As quite as a mouse—very quiet
> *E.g., everyone was talking and laughing. Only Mary was sitting aside as quiet as a mouse.*

As pale as a ghost—very pale

E.g., the movie was so scary that at the end all the audience looked as pale as a ghost.

As blind as a bat—not able to see

E.g., without his glasses, he is as blind as a bat.

As good as gold—a very well behaved person

E.g. Cathy has become a little disobedient. When she was a child, she was as good as gold.

As thick as a brick—slow to understand

E.g., Rita is as slow as a brick in math; she needs help.

As sober as a judge—completely sober

E.g., he was very lucky that he was as sober as a judge when the accident happened.

As black as thunder—look angry

E.g., Dad looked as black as thunder when he heard his daughter had failed the test.

As quick as flash—very fast and suddenly

E.g., when Maria opened her door, her cat ran out as quick as thunder.

As slippery as an eel—dishonest and untrustworthy

E.g., don't expect him to pay you what he promised. He is as slippery as an eel.

As smooth as velvet—very soft to the touch

E.g., Arba's skin is nice and smooth as velvet.

Straight as an arrow—in a straight direction

E.g., it was very easy to find your house. The road was straight as an arrow.

As heavy as lead—very heavy

> *E.g., after a two-hour walk, her legs were as heavy as lead.*

As bold as brass—shamelessly

> *E.g., she lied to me as bold as brass, not thinking twice about it.*

As pleased as punch—feel well; healthy

> *E.g., after the surgery, she was better and felt as pleased as punch.*

Exercises

(1) Match the idioms with their definitions.

1.	as sharp as a tack	a.	very calm and relaxed
2.	as hard as nails	b.	not clear
3.	as cool as a cucumber	c.	naïve
		d.	weak and sick
4.	as clean as a whistle	e.	totally sober
5.	as useless as a fifth wheel	f.	quick in understanding
6.	as clear as mud	g.	tough or no feeling
7.	as innocent as a lamb	h.	slow to understand
		i.	not needed
8.	as weak as a kitten	j.	clean
9.	as sober as a judge		
10.	as thick as a brick		

(2) Match a number in the first column with a letter in the second column.

1.	as comfortable	a.	as a skunk
2.	as easy	b.	as a beaver
3.	as drunk	c.	as night and day
4.	as regular	d.	as a rock
5.	as slow	e.	as pie
6.	as different	f.	as a snail
7.	as busy	g.	as clockwork
8.	as solid	h.	as an old shoe
9.	as plain	i.	as a picture
10.	as pretty	j.	as day

(3) Is the speaker happy or unhappy when:

1. he is as healthy as a horse
2. he is white as a sheet

3. his friend is hard as nails
4. his son is as stubborn as a mule
5. he is as free as a bird
6. he is as poor as a church mouse
7. he is as drunk as a skunk
8. what the teacher says is as clear as a bell
9. he is as useless as a fifth wheel
10. he is as thick as a brick

(4) Complete the sentences so that they are true.

1. I was as sick as a dog when _____
2. I was as white as a sheet when _____
3. I was as free as a bird _____
4. _____ was as drunk as a skunk
5. _____ as easy as pie for me
6. I was as busy as a beaver when _____
7. Me and _____ are as different as night and day
8. I was as cool as a cucumber when _____
9. I felt myself as useless as a fifth wheel when _____
10. I was as happy as a lark when _____
11. I was as pale as a ghost when _____
12. I was as hungry as a bear when _____

(5) Find someone who:

1. is as healthy as a horse
2. is as sick as a dog
3. is as quick as a bunny
4. is as hard as nails
5. is as sharp as a tack
6. is as nutty as a fruitcake
7. is as clever as a fox
8. is as strong as an ox

9. is as stubborn as a mule
10. is as weak as a kitten
11. is as slow as a snail
12. is as quiet as a mouse
13. is as different as night and day from you
14. is as cool as a cucumber
15. is as busy as a beaver
16. is as poor as a church mouse
17. is as happy as a lark
18. is as innocent as a lamb
19. is as blind as a bat without his glasses
20. is as sober as a judge

(6) Pair/group work: create your own situations using some of the comparison idioms.

NATURE

Break the ice—begin a conversation
E.g., Donna is very shy, and she finds it hard to break the ice.

Skate on thin ice—take a chance; to risk danger
E.g., I knew I was skating on thin ice by investing all my money in the restaurant.

The tip of the iceberg—a small part of a larger problem
E.g., she has a lot of problems. The one you know is only the tip of the iceberg.

Snowed under—have a lot of work to do
E.g., Jennifer has two big assignments due next Monday. She is snowed under.

Beat around the bush—talk without getting to the main point
E.g., Politicians often beat around the bush. They talk a lot but never get to the main point.

Make a mountain out of a molehill—make a big problem out of a small problem
E.g., my friend got so angry with me for being five minutes late. She made a mountain out of a molehill.

Bark up the wrong tree—waste your efforts by making the wrong choice
E.g., they were barking the wrong tree, blaming George for the accident.

Out of the woods—out of danger and trouble
E.g., after the accident, she was in the hospital for a week but is now out of the woods.

Over the hill—getting old
> *E.g., He used to run every day but has trouble now. He must be over the hill.*

Go down the hill—go down in numbers or quality
> *E.g., after September 11, many companies went down the hill.*

On the rocks—a relation or business experiencing difficulties
> *E.g., their marriage was on the rocks, but they had decided not to divorce until the children were grown up.*

Build castles in the air—daydream; make plans which will never come true
> *E.g., be realistic and don't build castles in the air.*

Clear the air—get rid of doubts or hard feelings
> *E.g., stop arguing. Clear the air first.*

Have one's nose in the air—be conceited
> *E.g., since she won the prize, she has her nose in the air.*

Up in the air—undecided; uncertain
> *E.g., I don't know what Helen is going to do. Things are sort of up in the air.*

Full of hot air—not keeping one's promises
> *E.g., many politicians are full of hot air. They don't keep their promises.*

Into thin air—completely disappear
> *E.g., their plans disappeared into thin air when their money was stolen.*

Air views—make your opinions known to other people
> *E.g., the new prime minister aired his views on television.*

Walk on air—very happy and proud
E.g., James will be walking on air if he passes the exam.

In the air—something is happening or about to happen
E.g., after many chilly days in May, spring is in the air.

A breath of fresh air—a nice change
E.g., having a little baby in the house is something different and a breath of fresh air.

A breeze—something very easy for a person to do
E.g., the exam is a breeze if you study hard.

Not have the foggiest idea—don't know or understand at all
E.g., I hadn't the foggiest idea what she was talking about.

Come rain or shine—no matter what
E.g., she promised to come to my party come rain or shine.

Rain on the parade--- someone spoils someone else's plans or pleasure
E.g., I am sorry to rain on your parade, but you can't smoke in the restaurant.

When it rains, it pours—a lot of bad things tend to happen at the same time
E.g., he lost his job and his car broke. When it rains, it pours.

Down in the dumps—feel sad
E.g., He looks down in the dumps today. Something must have happened to him.

Come down to earth—be realistic
E.g., I like your ideas, Tom, but you must come down to earth. We can't afford what you want.

Move heaven and earth to do something—make every effort to do something
E.g., she had to move heaven and earth to get the job she wanted.

Be bushed—tired or exhausted
E.g., After working overtime, I was bushed and went straight to bed.

Up the creek—in trouble; in a bad situation
E.g., Jane has been up the creek since she was fired.

Go sky high—go very high
E.g., after the hurricane, gas prices went sky high.

Pie in the sky—a plan that is really a dream
E.g., he wants to buy a brand new car, but at the moment it is only pie in the sky.

Praise to the sky—praise someone extravagantly
E.g., we all rolled our eyes when she praised her daughters to the sky.

Shoot the breeze—talk about unimportant matters, talk casually without purpose
E.g., My neighbor came over for a cup of coffee and it was nice to shoot the breeze with her for a couple of hours.

The sky is the limit—the possibilities are endless
E.g., after you graduate from law school, the sky is the limit.

A cloud on the horizon—a sign of trouble to come, a problem is expected to happen
E.g., There will be an increase in the subway tickets. This is another cloud in the horizon.

Promise the moon—promise that cannot be done
> *E.g., the politician promised the moon, but the voters knew his promises were unlikely.*

Over the moon—very happy
> *E.g., I was over the moon when Hannah was born.*

Ask/cry for the moon—ask for something you cannot possibly have
> *E.g., when you think of buying a Cadillac, you are crying for the moon.*

Chase rainbows—waste your time trying for something you can never have
> *E.g., the company president might be chasing rainbows trying to find proof to blame innocent people.*

Nature stop---a stop to use the toilet (usually during road travel)
> *E.g., It took us nine hours to get to New York including the nature stops.*

Weather the storm—pass safely through difficult times
> *E.g., many companies did not manage to weather the storm after September 11 and failed.*

Under the weather—feel sick
> *E.g., Susan didn't go to work because she was under the weather.*

The break of dawn—the earliest light of day
> *E.g., I'm always up for work at the break of dawn, even though the sun is barely out.*

Make someone's day—make someone happy
> *E.g., he made my day by giving me the news that I was qualified for the job.*

Begin to see daylight—begin to see the end of a long task
> *E.g., I was so busy, and with your help, I began to see daylight.*

In broad daylight—without trying to hide something
> *E.g., they robbed the bank in the broad daylight.*

Exercises

(1) Match the idioms with their definitions.

1.	skate on thin ice	a.	get rid of doubts or hard feelings
2.	break the ice		
3.	out of the woods	b.	very happy
4.	clear the air	c.	something easy to do
5.	a breath of fresh air	d.	exhausted
6.	a breeze	e.	a dream
7.	bushed	f.	to risk a danger
8.	pie in the sky	g.	a sign of trouble to come
9.	a cloud in the horizon		
		h.	out of danger
10.	over the moon j. a nice change	i.	begin a conversation

(2) Finish the idioms with one of the following words:

day, moon, iceberg, earth, breeze, mountain, sky, air

1. tip of the _____
2. make a _____ out of a molehill
3. praise to the _____
4. shoot the _____
5. come down to _____
6. the _____ is the limit
7. move heaven and _____
8. cry for the _____
9. full of hot _____
10. make someone's _____

(3) Is the speaker happy or unhappy when:

1. he is snowed under
2. he is out of the woods

3. he is over the hill
4. he is going down the hill
5. he is walking on air
6. his exam is a breeze
7. he is praised to the sky
8. he sees a cloud in the horizon
9. he is under the weather

(4) Fill in the blanks with the missing words:

1. snowed _____
2. _____ broad daylight
3. _____ the hill
4. go _____ the hill
5. walk _____ air
6. pie _____ the sky
7. praise _____ the sky
8. cry _____ the moon
9. _____ the break of dawn

(5) Complete the sentences so that they are true.

1. I was skating on thin ice when _____
2. I was snowed under when _____
3. They were barking the wrong tree when _____
4. I had to break the ice when _____
5. I was out of the woods when _____
6. _____ went down the hill.
7. I was walking on air when _____
8. _____was a breeze for me.
9. At the break of dawn _____

(6) Find someone who:

1. cries for the moon
2. gets up at the break of dawn

3.   is under the weather
4.   made your day yesterday
5.   is snowed under
6.   is over the hill
7.   is out of the woods
8.   has his nose in the air
9.   is up the creek

(7) Pair/group work: create your own situations using some of the nature idioms.

COLORS

Feel blue—feel sad

E.g., the first time I met her, she was feeling blue since she knew very few people in this city.

Out of the blue—unexpectedly

E.g., it was quite sunny when we went out, and then out of the blue, it started raining heavily.

Once in a blue moon—very rarely

E.g., I used to go to the bar every weekend, but now only once in a blue moon.

Cry the blues—complain because your friend or lover has gone

E.g., Tom is crying the blues because his girlfriend left him.

Baby blues—feeling sad after one gives birth

E.g., After she gave birth to her son, Kate had the baby blues. She was feeling sad.

Birthday blues—A state of depression due to the realization of getting older

E.g., today is Mary's birthday, but she doesn't seem happy. She's got the birthday blues.

Until you are blue in the face—until you are very tired or very aggravated

E.g., I called my friend until I was blue in the face. The line was busy.

True blue—faithful or loyal

E.g., Tom is true blue. He has been my best friend for fifteen years.

Between the devil and the deep blue sea—in a difficult situation

E.g., If we go out in the rain, we'll get wet. If we wait for the rain to stop, we'll be late for the meeting. We are between the devil and the deep blue sea.

The black market—the market where things are not controlled by the government or legal

E.g., He bought a gold Rolex watch on the black market for only $200.

Give a black eye—cause a loss of respect or a bad reputation for a person or organization

E.g., his unprepared speech gave him a black eye.

Pot calling the kettle black—blaming someone while having the same fault

E.g., Ben is always calling the kettle black when he blames his classmates for cheating because he does it too.

A black day—a day when something terrible happened

E.g., September 11 was a black day.

In black and white—very clear to understand

E.g., parking was included in the contract. It was stated in black and white.

In the black—in a good financial position

E.g., after many years our company was in the black.

Show one's true colors—reveal your real and usually bad character

E.g., we thought she was kind and generous, but she showed her true colors when she was caught stealing her friend's purse.

A red-letter day—memorable day; a special day
E.g., a wedding day is a red-letter day.

Caught red-handed—caught in the act of doing something wrong
E.g., the smuggler was caught red-handed with a kilo of cocaine.

Red tape—many official forms and rules
E.g., to get a birth certificate, you face a lot of red tape.

In the red—in a difficult financial situation
E.g., he continues to borrow money from the bank because his business is still in the red.

Paint the town red—have a celebration
E.g., on days off work for the national holidays, we paint the town red.

Roll out the red carpet—welcome an important or famous person with special treatment
E.g., we rolled the red carpet when the queen visited our city.

See red—become angry
E.g., when he told how he had broken his new bike, his father saw red.

Be in the pink—feel healthy
E.g., she had cancer a few years ago, but now she is in the pink.

Tickled pink—very happy
E.g., Bill was tickled pink when he had his first son.

Pink slip—a notice that informs you of termination from employment
E.g., Mike was always late to work, so the manager gave him the pink slip.

Green—inexperienced

E.g., Diana is still green at this job, so I'll have to give her a hand.

The grass is greener on the other side—other people's things seem to be better

E.g., "I wish I had a job like yours. It sounds more interesting than mine," I said.

"Yes, and I feel the same about you. The grass is always greener on the other side," she replied.

Have a green thumb—naturally good with plants

E.g., Kathy has a green thumb. Her plants always grow well.

Give someone the green light—give someone permission to do or start something

E.g., I was excited because my boss gave me the green light to buy new furniture for my office.

Green with envy—envious

E.g., when Gabriel bought his BMW, his friend who wanted one was green with envy.

White elephant—an expensive object purchased before but is no longer wanted or expensive to maintain

E.g., The little cottage we bought ten years ago is a white elephant. We spend a lot of money to maintain it.

A white lie—something that is not true but does not harm anyone

E.g., I didn't really like my neighbor's pie, but I had to tell her a white lie that it was very delicious.

A **white-collar crime**—a financial crime, such as stealing money secretly from people, companies, or government
E.g., her husband was involved in a white-collar crime at the bank.

White with fear—be very afraid
E.g., when she heard a strange noise in the kitchen at night, she was white with fear.

Yellow—afraid to defend; lacking courage
E.g., Don't think I am yellow, but I don't want to fight.

With flying colors—with great success; victoriously
E.g., Mira passed the test with flying colors.

Off color—rude or impolite
E.g., that joke you told us was off color and embarrassed me.

Exercises

(1) Match the idioms with their definitions.

1.	feel blue	a.	official forms
2.	in black and white	b.	become angry
3.	paint the town red	c.	inexperienced
4.	red tape	d.	lacking courage
5.	to be in the pink	e.	in good financial position
6.	green		
7.	in the black	f.	rude
8.	yellow	g.	have a celebration
9.	off color	h.	feel sad
10.	see red	i.	feel very well
		j.	very clear to understand

(2) Finish the following idioms.

1. out of the _____
2. _____ market
3. give a _____ eye
4. in black and _____
5. show one's true _____
6. caught _____ handed
7. paint the town _____
8. to have a _____ thumb
9. a _____ lie
10. _____ with envy

(3) Is the speaker happy or unhappy when:

1. cries the blues
2. he does something till he is blue in the face
3. somebody gives him a black eye
4. sees red

5. has a white elephant in his house
6. he is yellow
7. he has the green light to do something
8. he is green with envy
9. he is green
10. he buys something at the black market

(4) Fill in the blanks:

1. _____ of the blue
2. until you are blue _____ the face
3. _____ the devil and the deep blue sea
4. _____ the black
5. the grass is greener _____ the other side
6. roll _____ the red carpet
7. _____ black and white
8. to be _____ the pink
9. to be white _____ fear
10. _____ flying colors

(5) Complete the sentences so that they are true.

1. I felt blue when _____
2. _____ once in a blue moon.
3. I was between the devil and the deep blue sea when _____
4. _____ until I was blue in the face
5. My friend cried the blues when _____
6. You can buy _____ on the black market.
7. _____ is a red-letter day.
8. We painted the town red when _____
9. We rolled out the red carpet when _____
10. _____ you face a lot of red tape.

(6) Find someone who:

1. feels blue
2. cries the blues
3. buys things on the black market
4. has been given a black eye
5. is in the red
6. is in the black
7. has been caught red-handed
8. is in the pink
9. tells white lies
10. has a green thumb

(7) Pair/group work: create your own situations using some of the color idioms.

NUMBERS

Have second thoughts—change one's mind or opinion about something

E.g., Susan wanted to study medicine, but now she is having second thoughts.

Second to none—the best

E.g., Prince Park restaurant is second to none. You get the best food there.

Second nature—easy and natural to someone

E.g., fixing cars is second nature to my friend.

To put two and two together—come to a conclusion about something; to finally understand

E.g., trying to get a job without speaking the language was a waste of time, so she put two and two together and went to an English class.

Put two and two together and make five—To draw the wrong conclusion

E.g., She told Rita's mother that Rita had brought her boyfriend home the night before, but she had put two and two together and made five because the young man was her cousin.

Of two minds—having trouble making a decision

E.g., Ben is of two minds about his future: should he study to be a doctor or a lawyer?

A stitch in time saves nine—s small repair may prevent a large one

E.g., you should go to the doctor for your cough. It may turn into a cold later—a stitch in time saves nine.

Nine lives—lucky to survive

E.g., Linda had a bad accident but is alive. She has nine lives.

Nine times out of ten—almost always

    E.g., I like to eat out nine times out of ten.

Take forty winks—sleep for a short time during the day

    E.g., Tom went to bed at three in the morning and took forty winks on the train to work.

In the eleventh hour—just before it's too late; at the last minute

    E.g., I arrived at the airport in the eleventh hour; the gate was just closing as I boarded.

Five o'clock shadow—the stubble of a man who hasn't shaved

    E.g., after staying in the hospital for two days, he looked tired and had a five o'clock shadow.

One in a million—unique; very special

    E.g., Thanks for your great help, Lisa. You are one in a million.

Of the first water—of the finest quality

    E.g., this is a very fine pearl; it is of the first water.

First thing's first—the most important things must be taken care of first

    E.g., Do your homework now, and then go out and play later—first thing's first.

Back to square one—back to the first step; start from scratch

    E.g., after the hurricane ruined their house, they had to go back to square one.

At first sight—after a quick look

    E.g., at first sight this job seemed okay, but now I think differently.

It takes two to tango--- if two people were involved in a bad situation, both must be responsible.
E.g., Her husband is awful; they fight all the time. However, it takes two to tango.

Two is company; three is a crowd—a group of three people is uncomfortable
E.g., I asked my divorced friend to come with me and my husband to the movie, but she said, "Thanks, but two is company; three is a crowd."

Two wrongs don't make a right—it's never right to do wrong to another person who has hurt you before
E.g., that boy pushed me yesterday, but I'm not doing the same to him today—two wrongs don't make a right.

Get the third degree—questioned in great detail for a long time
E.g., every time Matthew comes home late, he gets the third degree about where he's been.

Six of one, half a dozen of the other—no difference; either choice is okay
E.g., I don't care whether we go to the beach or to the park. It's six of one, half a dozen of the other.

Sixth sense—a feeling something will happen
E.g., my sixth sense knew it was him when the phone rang.

Sixty-four-thousand-dollar question—very important question
E.g., the sixty-four-thousand-dollar question for my students is, "When can you speak English fluently?"

In seventh heaven—extremely happy
E.g., Helen was in seventh heaven when she graduated from college at the top of her class.

On cloud nine—extremely happy
E.g.,

At sixes and sevens—confused or undecided
E.g., many young people are at sixes and sevens about what to do in the future.

All at sea—confused or undecided
E.g., before deciding to immigrate, Ron was all at sea.

Catch-22—a difficult situation from which you cannot escape because there are conditions that block the escape
E.g., she can't get a permanent job unless she joins the union, and she can't join the union unless she gets a permanent job—it's a Catch-22.

Ten to one—very likely to happen
E.g., ten to one the meeting will be cancelled and we'll go home.

Five finger discount ---get something without paying, steal
E.g., I saw a very young man wearing an expensive Rolex watch. Maybe he got it with a five finger discount.

Five o'clock shadow----kind of stubble on the face of a man who hasn't shaved for a day or two
E.g., When he came home in the morning after the night shift, he looked tired and had a five o'clock shadow.

Have (someone's) number—be able to understand someone
> E.g., I have that woman's number. She is a liar and unreliable.

Number cruncher—an accountant
> E.g., Mary's husband is a number cruncher, working on people's taxes.

Talk nineteen to the dozen—speak quickly and endlessly
> E.g., you know when Fiona is excited about something because she talks nineteen to the dozen.

Third time is a charm—the third time is lucky
> E.g., I've failed twice before, but my driving instructor is sure I can do it next time—the third time is a charm.

24/7—all the time
> E.g., Karen thinks of her business plans 24/7; they are never out of her mind.

Look after number one—look after yourself
> E.g., Looking after number one is sometimes selfish.

Exercises

(1) Match the idioms with their definitions.

1.	have second thoughts	a.	easy and natural to someone
2.	second to none	b.	have trouble making a decision
3.	in the eleventh hour		
4.	at first sight	c.	an accountant
5.	of two minds	d.	start from scratch
6.	number cruncher	e.	unique
7.	of first water	f.	the best
8.	second nature	g.	of the finest quality
9.	back to square one	h.	change one's mind
10.	one in a million	i.	at the last minute
		j.	after a quick look

(2) Finish the following idioms.

1. put _____ and together
2. of _____ minds
3. a stitch in time saves _____
4. take _____ winks
5. it takes _____ to tango
6. _____ wrongs don't make a right
7. _____ of one, half a _____ of the other
8. at sixes and _____
9. talk _____ to the dozen
10. _____ time is a charm

(3) Is the speaker happy or unhappy when:

1. he is of two minds
2. he takes forty winks
3. his friend is one in a million
4. he has to go back to square one

5. he arrives somewhere in the eleventh hour
6. he has a sixth sense
7. he gets the third degree
8. his friend talks nineteen to the dozen
9. he is in seventh heaven
10. he is at sixes and sevens

(4) Fill in the blanks:

1. second _____ none
2. a stitch _____ time saves nine
3. _____ the eleventh hour
4. back _____ square one
5. _____ first sight
6. _____ the first water
7. one _____ a million
8. _____ cloud nine
9. _____ sixes and sevens
10. _____ two minds

(5) Complete the sentences so that they are true.

1. I had second thoughts when _____
2. _____ is second nature.
3. I am of two minds about _____
4. I had nine lives when _____
5. I usually take forty winks when _____
6. At first sight I _____
7. I had to go back to square one when _____
8. I was in seventh heaven when _____
9. I was at sixes and sevens when _____
10. I had a sixth sense when _____

(6) Find someone who:

1. is of two minds about something
2. is one in a million
3. has nine lives
4. has been back to square one
5. has a sixth sense
6. has bought something of the first water
7. has gotten the third degree
8. is in seventh heaven
9. is at sixes and sevens about something

(7) Pair/group work: create your own situations using some of the number idioms.

LOVE AND WAR

Love at first sight—love between two people who see one another for the first time

E.g., it was love at first sight when they met, but it didn't last long.

Ask for someone's hand—ask for permission to marry someone

E.g., Cathy was happy when Alex got down on his knees and asked for her hand.

Tie the knot—get married

E.g., after dating for two years, Jim and Jess decided to tie the knot.

Beauty is in the eye of the beholder—what isn't beautiful to one person may be beautiful to another

E.g., Dave's parents didn't like his girlfriend, but he said, "Beauty is in the eye of the beholder."

Beauty is only skin deep—don't judge a person by physical features

E.g., we all advised Jess not to date Tom just because he was handsome, since beauty is only skin deep. He has such bad habits that she will later regret her decision.

Made for each other—well-suited romantically

E.g., Mr. and Mrs. Osborn were made for each other. They are such a lovely couple!

Out of sight, out of mind—you don't think about someone when you can no longer see them

E.g., when Tom went to war, his girlfriend married someone else—out of sight, out of mind!

Have one's heart go out to someone—have compassion for someone
E.g., when I heard about what had happened to Dave and how sad he was, my heart went out to him.

Give the bride away—accompany the bride to the groom in a wedding ceremony
E.g., Mr. Brown is ill. Who will give the bride away?

Walk down the aisle—get married
E.g., when Dora was walking down the aisle, she looked gorgeous.

Hear wedding bells—someone is getting ready to get married
E.g., when I saw Toni and Jenny in a jewelers store I said, "I hear wedding bells."

Bury the hatchet—stop fighting and make peace
E.g., after many hours of fighting, they decided to bury the hatchet.

Lay down one's arms—stop fighting in a war
E.g., when the order came to lay down their arms, the war was over.

Be on good terms—be friendly; have good relations
E.g., We have been on good terms with our neighbors for a long time.

Kiss and make up---become friends again after an argument or a fight
E.g. The two friends had an argument, but they were quick to kiss and make up.

Lose one's heart—fall in love

E.g., it's clear that Maria has lost her heart to Raymond and she is totally in love.

Take sides—support a person or an argument

E.g., you always take my sister's side when I have a fight with her.

Hold out an olive branch—say or do something to indicate that you want to end a disagreement

E.g., Jack an argument with his colleague, but the next day he held out an olive branch to him.

Mend a relationship—improve a relationship that has been on the rocks

E.g., Diane wants a divorce, but her husband is trying to mend the relationship.

Hit it off—relate well; be friends immediately

E.g., Dona and me hit it off the very first day we met and have been friends since.

Go steady—date only one person

E.g., Tom and Jane are going steady. They may get married next year.

An old flame—a previous boyfriend or girlfriend

E.g., "I didn't know Helen knew Carlos," I said.
"Oh, yes, he is an old flame of hers," she said.

Get a crush—feel romantic

E.g., when she was a high school student, she had a crush on her math teacher.

Love is blind—people do not see the faults in their lovers
E.g., how will she marry a man with a bad habit of gambling? I guess love is blind.

A knockout—a very attractive person
E.g., when I was dating my husband, everyone said he was a knockout.

Break someone's heart—cause somebody to feel very sad and lonely
E.g., she broke Tom's heart by leaving him.

Break up—come to an end, especially by separating
E.g., no one knows why they broke up after so many years together.

Stand someone up—break a date; not appear at the appointed time and place
E.g., Tom got so upset when Linda stood him up.

Blind date—go out with someone that you have not met before
E.g., Kate met Tom on a blind date, and they got married six months later.

Bite the bullet—be brave and calm in a difficult situation
E.g., he was told to bite the bullet before the operation.

Stick to your guns—refuse to change your opinion despite pressure
E.g., don't give in this time, Chris. Stick to your guns.

A losing battle—something that cannot be accomplished
E.g., she tried hard to take the TOEFL, but it was a losing battle.

Armed to teeth—lots of weapons or items to do a task; prepared to fight or defend
E.g., when we went big game hunting, we were armed to teeth.

Hold a grudge—continue to hold resentment
E.g., after the fight, they held a grudge against each other for years.

Pick a quarrel— start an argument with someone
E.g., are you trying to pick a quarrel with me?

Pick on someone—be very critical of someone
E.g., why are you always picking on me?

Up in arms—be angry about something
E.g., Watch out for Emma. She is up in arms because someone ripped her son's new jacket.

Cross swords—disagree and argue
E.g., when he grew up, he started crossing swords with his father.

Fight tooth and nail—fight very hard
E.g., after fighting tooth and nail with the enemy, our army won the battle.

Drop the bombshell—give unexpected information that amazes or shocks
E.g., everyone was shocked when Mary dropped the bombshell that she had won one million dollars.

Go like a bomb—quickly become a great success
E.g., sales of his new book are going like a bomb.

Fight fire with fire—fight with the same weapon the enemy uses

E.g., when debating about this issue during the electoral campaign, fight fire with fire. If they use statistics, you also use statistics.

Kiss of death—something that is certain to cause failure

E.g., rain is the kiss of death for an outdoor BBQ.

An old warhorse—someone who has been around for a long time

E.g., Gary is going to retire soon. He is an old warhorse.

Exercises

(1) Match the idioms with their definitions.

1.	ask for someone's hand	a.	date only one person
2.	tie the knot	b.	fall in love
3.	lose one's heart	c.	improve a relationship
4.	bury the hatchet	d.	feel romantic about someone
5.	mend a relationship		
6.	go steady	e.	a previous boy/girlfriend
7.	get a crush on someone	f.	start an argument
		g.	relate well
8.	hit it off	h.	get married
9.	pick a quarrel with someone	i.	ask for permission to marry someone
10.	an old flame	j.	stop fighting

(2) Finish the following idioms.

1. beauty is in the _____ of the beholder
2. a real _____ throb
3. beauty is only _____ deep
4. give the _____ away
5. hold out an _____ branch to someone
6. break someone's _____
7. a losing _____
8. hold a grudge _____ someone
9. cross _____ with someone
10. drop the _____

(3) Is the speaker happy or unhappy when he/she:

1. is asking for someone's hand
2. ties the knot with someone
3. meets a real heartthrob

4. gives the bride away
5. buries the hatchet
6. is on good terms with his boss
7. breaks someone's heart
8. crosses swords with his friend
9. meets an old flame
10. is up in arms

(4) Fill in the blanks with one of the following prepositions:

with, to, out, down, off, at, up

1. have one's heart go _____ to someone
2. _____ of sight, _____ of mind
3. lay one's arms _____
4. get along _____ someone
5. hold _____ an olive branch to someone
6. hit it _____
7. stand someone _____
8. armed _____ teeth
9. pick someone _____
10. fight fire _____ fire

(5) Complete the sentences so that they are true.

1. _____ is a real heartthrob.
2. I lost my heart to _____
3. I buried the hatched when _____
4. I am on good terms with _____
5. I had a crush on _____
6. _____ and I hit it off.
7. I broke someone's heart when _____
8. I had to stick to my guns when _____
9. I have never held a grudge against _____

10. I was shocked when he dropped the bombshell that _____

(6) Find someone who:

1. has fallen in love at first sight
2. has lost his/her heart
3. is a real heartthrob
4. has given the bride away
5. has mended a relationship
6. has broken your heart
7. has had a losing battle
8. holds a grudge against you
9. has bitten the bullet

(7) Pair/group work: create your own situations using some of the love and war idioms.

...AND...

Sick and tired—annoyed

E.g., we are all sick and tired of this weather.

Hit-and-run—an accident in which the driver leaves the scene of the collision

E.g., he was punished when they found out that his car was involved in a hit-and-run.

Spick and span—very clean

E.g., she is always doing housework. Everything in her house is spick and span.

Ups and downs—good fortune and bad fortune

E.g., all of us have our ups and downs in life.

Wine and dine—treat someone to expensive food and drink

E.g., our business trip was great. They wined and dined us all week.

Black and blue—badly bruised

E.g., When I was riding my bike and fell down I had some black and blue marks on my legs.

Ins and outs—all the details

E.g., they hired him right away because he knew the ins and out of computers.

Out and about—out and at different places

E.g., when we visited England, most of the time we were out and about.

Flesh and blood—a relative

E.g., My grandfather left his money to his own flesh and blood.

Pins and needles—very nervous and anxious
> *E.g., while they were interviewing my husband, I was on pins and needles.*

Nooks and crannies—hidden or little-known places
> *E.g., the police searched every nook and cranny to find the criminal, but they couldn't.*

Break and enter—enter illegally, force oneself into a place
> *E.g., There was no need to break and enter in the house. The door was open.*

Come and go—existing only for a short time
> *E.g., newspapers come and go, so everything written in them will soon be forgotten.*

Thrills and spills—an experience that is exciting and full of surprises
> *E.g., our trip to Africa was all thrills and spills.*

Body and soul—in all aspects of one's being, both physically and mentally
> *E.g., he devoted himself body and soul to his job.*

High and mighty—better than other people
> *E.g., after she married the president, she acted high and mighty.*

Smoke and mirrors—false impressions
> *E.g., his speech about new projects is just smoke and mirrors. The company is actually going bankrupt.*

Odds and ends—small items left over
> *E.g., there had been good fruit at the store, but when I got there it was too late and there were only odds and ends.*

Peace and quiet—calm and silent
E.g., we enjoyed some peace and quiet when the party was over and twenty-five guests went home.

Milk and honey—a time in which you are very content and have plenty of money
E.g., it was milk and honey when our business grew and we made so much money.

Up and about—healthy and moving about
E.g., Mira is getting better. She should be up and about soon.

Such and such—someone or something whose name has been forgotten or should not be said
E.g., Helen said that such and such had told her about the rumors that the manager was going to retire.

Skin and bones—very thin
E.g., Bill has lost so much weight. He is all skin and bones.

By trial and error—try all ways until you reach success
E.g., I learned how to use the computer by trial and error.

Neck and neck—exactly even, especially in a race or a contest
E.g., In the previous campaign, the Conservatives was neck and neck with the Liberals.

Betwixt and between—not able to choose one or the other
E.g., which one should I choose: laptop or desktop? I am betwixt and between.

Bits and pieces—small pieces of different kind
E.g., I put all the bits and pieces away when my grandchildren left.

Cash and carry—paying by cash and no delivery service
E.g., the furniture store told us that buying there was cash and carry, so we needed a truck.

Bright and early—very early in the morning
E.g., We have a long drive tomorrow, so, we better hit the road bright and early.

By and by—after a period of time has passed
E.g., By and by, the little boy became a tall, handsome man.

By and large—generally; usually
E.g., by and large, learning English needs a lot of work.

By fits and starts—with much stopping and starting; irregularly
E.g., by fits and starts, the old car finally got us to town.

Hit and miss—learn by correcting errors
E.g., I finally learned to make a pie by hit and miss.

Touch and go—between life and death
E.g., he recovered from his heart attack, but it was touch and go for some time.

Thick and thin—for better and worse; during good and bad times
E.g., Helen is a true friend. She stays with me through thick and thin.

Head and shoulders—superior by a great deal
E.g., Mary is head and shoulders above her classmates.

Grin and bear—be brave and calm in a difficult situation
E.g., after the surgery, she was told to grin and bear it.

High and dry—leave someone helpless
> *E.g., she took all the money out of the bank and left her husband high and dry.*

Live and learn—the more you live, the more you learn, learn from experience and from mistakes
> *E.g., I didn't know that beans are good for your cholesterol. I never ate them. Well, live and learn!*

Huffing and puffing—breathing hard
> *E.g., after we got to the top of the hill, everyone was huffing and puffing.*

Down and gloom—bad news
> *E.g., I have heard many of those down-and-gloom stories about the end of the world.*

Wear and tear—damage from longtime use
> *E.g., I bought a new carpet because the one we had got a lot of wear and tear.*

Long and hard—for a long time
> *E.g., look, John, I've thought long and hard about our relationship and it's not going to work if you continue to work until ten o'clock at night.*

Safe and sound—safe after an illness or accident
> *E.g., I was happy to hear that my friend was not hurt when she had an accident. When I saw her, she was safe and sound.*

Rise and shine—a command to someone to get up
> *E.g., time to leave, Tom—rise and shine.*

Right and left—from every side
> *E.g., when he became famous, invitations were coming from right and left.*

One and all—everyone

E.g., One and all came to meet my fiancé.

Back and forth—going from one place to another and back again

E.g., Peter got a job one hour from town. Every day he takes the train back and forth.

Tried and tested—tried by many other people and proved to be true

E.g., when I get a cold, I go to bed with whisky and honey. The next day I am fine. It's a tried-and-tested remedy.

Forgive and forget—forget arguments with my friends

E.g., if I have an argument with someone, I always try to forgive and forget. It's the only way to keep friendships.

Cut and dried—the decision is final and unlikely to be changed

E.g., The City has made some cut and dried decisions about the property tax.

Chalk and cheese—very different from one another

E.g., though they are brothers, they are as different as chalk and cheese.

High and low—everywhere

E.g., I can't find my car keys anywhere. I've searched high and low.

Alive and kicking—still active and successful

E.g., though my father is seventy-eight, he is alive and kicking.

By leaps and bounds—great progress

E.g., Lidia's English has improved by leaps and bounds since she went to an ESL class.

First and foremost—what is most important

E.g., if you are going to start a business, first and foremost you need some financial advice.

Give and take—if you help, you expect to be helped

E.g., all successful relations are a matter of give and take.

Born and bred—born and raised

E.g., my friend's husband is Italian born and bred in Italy.

Pick and choose—have the right to choose

E.g., if you have no experience, you are not really in a position to pick and choose.

Fair and square—done honestly or without cheating

E.g., we won the game fair and square. We followed the rules.

Meat and potatoes—the most important and basic need

E.g., getting a job is the meat-and-potatoes issue for many immigrants.

Kiss and tell—talk on TV, the radio, etc. about a relationship you have had

E.g., she did a kiss-and-tell interview concerning the actor for a local TV station.

Dead and buried—something no longer considered; a settled issue

E.g., Rose no longer insisted on marrying Pedro. Her parents considered this dead and buried.

Thick and fast—in great quantity or large numbers

E.g., when he became famous, invitations were pouring in thick and fast.

Null and void—not valid; cancelled

E.g., the results of the elections were declared null and void.

Song and dance—an excuse for something that hides the truth

E.g., Ann is always late and when she comes, she gives me a song and dance about getting stuck in the traffic.

Exercises

(1) Match the idioms with their definitions.

1.	spick and span	a.	very nervous
2.	black and blue	b.	false impression
3.	pins and needles	c.	exactly even
4.	smoke and mirrors	d.	small pieces
5.	skin and bones	e.	between life and death
6.	neck and neck	f.	for better and worse
7.	bits and pieces	g.	bad news
8.	touch and go	h.	very clean
9.	thick and thin	i.	very thin
10.	down and gloom	j.	badly bruised

(2) Match a number in the first column with a letter in the second column

1.	sick		a.	ends
2.	wine		b.	miss
3.	break		c.	large
4.	hit		d.	tear
5.	odds	and	e.	dine
6.	high		f.	carry
7.	milk		g.	tired
8.	by		h.	enter
9.	cash		i.	low
10.	wear		j.	honey

(3) Is the speaker happy or unhappy when:

1. he is sick and tired
2. everything in her house is spick and span
3. he is betwixt and between
4. he makes something by hit and miss
5. he was left high and dry

6. he hears some down-and-gloom stories
7. his sofa has a lot of wear and tear
8. he forgives and forgets
9. his parents are alive and kicking
10. he goes shopping and find only odds and ends

(4) Pair/group work: create your own situations using some of ...and... idioms.

CLOTHES

DRITA SKILJA

Be in someone else's shoes—be in the place of someone else
E.g., when Helen won the lottery, we all said we wanted to be in her shoes.

Have the shoe on the other foot—experience the opposite from a previous situation
E.g., Mira used to be a teacher in my school. Now she is our manager. She now has the show on the other foot.

On a shoe string—live with very little money
E.g., some university students live on a shoe string, as they have to work part time to pay for their tuition.

Fill someone's shoes—take someone's job or position
E.g., they are looking for someone to fill the manager's shoes.

Too big for one's boots—feel more important than one really is
E.g., after he was made captain of the team, Frank began to get too big for his boots.

Lick someone's boots—obey with servility somebody who has authority over you
E.g., I am not going to lick his boots to get a promotion.

Die with one's boots on—die while still leading an active life
E.g., it was quite a shock when her dad passed away. He was still working and never got sick. He died with his boots on.

Given/get the boot—told that the job or a relationship you have with someone is over
E.g., he told me that he has lost his job. He was given the boot.

Pull yourself up by your own bootstraps—improve yourself without being helped by others
E.g., After he failed in the exam, Jeff studied hard and he pulled himself up by his bootstraps. He passed with great results.

Dressed to kill—dressed in one's best clothes and looking good
E.g., Bob went to a party dressed to kill in his new black suit and red tie.

Dressed up to the nines—dressed in one's best clothes and looking good
E.g., I just saw Bob dressed up to the nines. He must be going to a wedding.

All dressed up with nowhere to go—wearing your best clothes and ready for a party, ceremony, etc., but something happens and ruins your plans
E.g., we were all set to go to the picnic when suddenly it started to pour. We were all dressed up with nowhere to go.

Keep one's shirt on—Be patient
E.g., I'll be with you in a minute—just keep your shirt on.

Give the shirt off your back—be very generous and willing to help people as much as you can
E.g., everyone knows how generous she is. She would give the shirt off her back to anyone in need.

Lose one's shirt—lose money
E.g., Ann invested a lot of money in stocks and lost her shirt.

A stuffed shirt—someone who is too formal even in casual situations
E.g., Tom is such a stuffed shirt. Even at a picnic he would wear a tie.

Roll up your sleeves—get ready to work
E.g., exam time is coming. I have to roll up my sleeves and start studying.

Take one's hat off to someone—show respect and appreciation
E.g., I take my hat off to my parents for everything they have done for me.

Tip one's hat to someone—show respect and appreciation
E.g., I think so highly of my dad. I tip my hat to him for his gentleness and thoughtfulness.

Pass the hat—collect money to contribute for someone's illness, celebration, etc.
E.g., we passed the hat to buy a gift for John when he retired.

Talk through one's hat—not know what you are talking about
E.g., don't listen to him. He is talking through his hat.

Keep something under one's hat—keep it a secret
E.g., He won one million dollars in a lottery, but he kept it under his hat and no one found out.

Hang on to your hat—prepare for a sudden surprise or shock
E.g., Hang on to your hat. I got accepted at the Law School.

At the drop of a hat—quickly or without hesitation
E.g., Scott likes to argue. He will argue at the drop of a hat.

A feather in one's cap—something you are proud of
E.g., passing the driving test was a real feather in my cap.

Hot under the collar—angry
E.g., Mike got hot under the collar because he missed the train for an important meeting.

Hand in glove—very close
E.g., John is really hand in glove with his boss.

Fit like a glove—fit very well
E.g., my new shoes fit like a glove.

Get ants in one's pants—become nervous or agitated
E.g., I always get ants in my pants before a test.

Catch somebody with their pants down—discover someone in the act of doing something secret
E.g., Some city hall councilors were using tax money as their own, but the press caught them with their pants down and told everyone.

Wear the pants—the person in charge
E.g., she wears the pants in her family. Everyone does what she says.

A kick in the pants—a strong message of encouragement
E.g., all she needs is a kick in the pants to get her going.

Hit someone below the belt—attack someone in an unfair way
E.g., the remark they gave him in the meeting was not fair. They hit him below the belt after all the great work he had done.

Wash one's dirty laundry in public—make a public spectacle of family quarrels
E.g., Linda always talks about her arguments and fights with her husband. Why does she always washe her dirty laundry in public?

Tied to someone's apron strings—being controlled by a stronger person
E.g., Bill is still tied to his wife's apron strings. He will always ask her what he should wear.

Cut from the same cloth—similar; of the same nature
E.g., Linda and her friend Julie are cut from the same cloth. The have the same hobbies and dislike the same things.

Change/turn your coat—change sides; betray a group to join another
E.g., they all hate him. He turns his coat and joins whatever political party wins the elections.

Cut your coat according to your cloth—avoid spending more than you earn
E.g., You can't ask for a fancy car at the moment. You just have a part-time job. Cut the coat according to your cloth.

Exercises

(1) Match the idioms with their definitions.

1. fill someone's shoes
2. lose one's shirt
3. below the belt
4. fit like a glove
5. on a shoe string
6. at the drop of a hat
7. dressed to kill
8. a feather in one's cap
9. get ants in one's pants
10. too big for one's boots

a. with very little money
b. dressed in one's best
c. quickly
d. take someone's job
e. something you are proud of
f. become agitated
g. fit very well
h. unfair remark
i. lose a lot of money
j. feeling more important than one really is

(2) Fill in the blanks with one of the following words:

shoe, shirt, pants, linen, glove, cap, apron, hat, collar

1. keep one's _____ on
2. talk through one's _____
3. tied to someone's _____ strings
4. keep something under one's _____
5. a feather in one's _____
6. hot under the _____
7. wash one's dirty _____ in public
8. get ants in one's _____
9. fit like a _____
10. have one's _____ on the other foot

(3) Is the speaker happy or unhappy when:

1. he fills his manager's shoes
2. he lives on a shoestring
3. he is dressed to kill
4. he loses his shirt
5. someone takes their hat off to him
6. he is hot under the collar
7. he buys something that fits like a glove
8. he is given a remark below the belt
9. he is hand in glove with his boss
10. he has a feather in his cap

(4) Fill in the gaps with the following prepositions:

in, through, on, with, for, under, below, at

1. too big _____ one's boots
2. _____ a shoe string
3. keep one's shirt _____
4. talk _____ one's hat
5. keep something _____ one's hat
6. have the shoe _____ the other foot
7. _____ the drop of a hat
8. hot _____ the collar
9. hand _____ glove _____ someone
10. _____ the belt

(5) Complete the sentences so that they are true.

1. I have always wanted to be in _____ shoes.
2. _____ began to get too big for his boots.
3. I had to live on a shoe string when _____
4. I asked my friend to keep _____ under her hat.
5. I take my hat off to _____
6. I lost my shirt when _____

7. I was dressed to kill when _____
8. I tried to keep my shirt on when _____
9. I want to fill _____ shoes.
10. _____ is a feather in my cap.

(6) Find someone who:

1. wants to be in your shoes
2. is too big for his shoes
3. has the shoe on the other foot
4. has filled the manager's shoes
5. is living on a shoestring
6. is always dressed to kill
7. has lost his shirt
8. is a stuffed shirt
9. is tied to his mother's apron strings
10. is hand in glove with his boss

(7) Pair/group work: create your own situations using some of the clothes idioms.

HOME

On the house—free because it is paid by the owner/host

E.g., *you'll have to come in and see our restaurant. Bring some friends and I'll cook a special dinner—on the house, of course.*

People who live in glass houses should not throw stones—don't criticize other people when you yourself have faults

E.g., *"It's the second time you are late," I said.*

"Hey, you are never on time yourself! People who live in glass houses should not throw stones," she replied.

In the doghouse—facing punishment for doing something wrong

E.g., *children are often in the doghouse with their mother after a mess.*

Get on with someone like a house on fire—get along very well with someone

E.g., *the manager was such a sweet person. We got on like a house on fire.*

Bring the house down—to excite and entertain the audience very successfully

E.g., *the president's speech was so electrifying that it brought the house down.*

Put one's own house in order—sort out one's own problems first

E.g., *the new party leader must put his party's house in order before criticizing the opposition.*

Hit home—make someone realize something

E.g., *the problems with the economy really hit home when she lost her job.*

Nothing to write home about—nothing special or impressive
   E.g., this new job title sounds very impressive, but it's really nothing to write home about.

Keep the home fires burning—keep things going at one's home or other location
   E.g., the manager stays at the office and keeps the home fires burning.

A broken home—one's parents are divorced
   E.g., I feel very sorry for Ina because she comes from a broken home. Her parents divorced when she was six years old.

The lights are on but nobody is home—not listening; not at all there, even when you are looking at the person who is talking to you
   E.g., I explained the grammar to my students, but they were not listening. The lights were on but nobody was home.

Come down on someone like a ton of bricks—criticize someone very strongly
   E.g., when she found out that I had left early, my manager came down on me like a ton of bricks.

Sugar daddy—a rich older man who dates and spends a lot on younger women
   E.g., Her parents were not happy with their daughter marrying a sugar daddy.

Trophy wife—a younger, beautiful woman who marries a much older, rich husband
   E.g., After his divorce, the Prime Minister married a trophy wife for his social position.

A bed of roses—an easy life; a pleasant place to work or stay

E.g., He was disappointed when he immigrated to Canada because he thought life there was a bed of roses.

Call someone on the carpet—reprimand a person for doing something wrong

E.g., just because of a computer error he had made, the boss called him on the carpet.

Blood on the carpet—trouble in the company, often resulting in someone losing their job

E.g., the manager was so upset with the poor performance of some of his employees. He announced a meeting, and we all knew there was blood on the carpet.

Sweep under the carpet—cover up; hide a mistake

E.g., he can't sweep his mistake under the carpet because people know about it.

Pull the carpet out from under someone's feet—suddenly stop supporting or helping someone

E.g., he pulled the carpet from under our feet by saying he was offered a better job.

A watched pot never boils—concentration on a problem will not help solve it

E.g., Helen was waiting eagerly for her vocation to come, but a watched pot never boils.

Familiarity breeds contempt—knowing a person too closely can lead to bad feelings

E.g., They were good friends for many years. Finally they got into a big argument and became enemies. Familiarity breeds contempt.

Get up on the wrong side of the bed—wake up in a bad
mood
> *E.g., when she doesn't sleep well at night, she gets up on the
> wrong side of the bed.*

Skeletons in the closet—secrets from your past which you
try not to show to other people
> *E.g., Mary married her husband and soon she learned that he
> had been in jail two times before. How would she know what
> skeletons he had in the closet.*

Come out of the closet—make oneself public after being in
a state of secrecy
> *E.g., more and more gay people are coming out of the closet.*

Have a bun in the oven—pregnant
> *E.g., my friend's daughter has put on a lot of weight;
> everyone says she has a bun in the oven.*

On the shelf—no longer active or of use
> *E.g., her father helps her with the gardening so that he does
> not feel on the shelf.*

Throw in the towel—accept defeat and loss
> *E.g., We all thought it was better for the prime minister to
> throw in the towel after the financial scandal.*

A wet blanket—a person who doesn't enjoy activities and
keeps others from enjoying them
> *E.g., don't be such a wet blanket. We'll have fun at the party.*

On the tiles—enjoying oneself in a wild manner, dancing,
drinking, etc.
> *E.g., after the exams were over, all the students had a night
> on the tiles.*

One brick short of a load—stupid or crazy

E.g., He must be one brick short of a load deciding to go swimming in the lake in such freezing weather.

Twist/turn the knife in the wound—make someone who is annoyed even more annoyed

E.g., just to turn the knife in the wound, she told me she had seen my ex-boyfriend with a new woman.

Go under the knife—have a medical operation

E.g., my friend had kidney stones and she had to go under knife.

A new broom sweeps clean—an employee who works hard on the first day or two

E.g., at the end of my first hard day of work in the company, everyone said, "A new broom sweeps clean."

Talk to a brick wall—speak but there is no response

E.g., are you listening to me, or I am talking to a brick wall?

Everything but the kitchen sink—almost everything

E.g., when we went camping, we took everything but the kitchen sink.

Go through the roof—become very angry

E.g., his father will go through the roof when he sees his car mirror broken.

Hit the ceiling—become very angry

E.g., my neighbor hit the ceiling when her son failed the exams.

A roof over your head—a place to live

E.g., after the hurricane, thousands of people had no roofs over their heads.

Go to the wall—do everything you can to help someone, even risking yourself
E.g., parents are willing to go to the wall for their children and do everything they can to make them happy.

Between you and me and the wall—in great confidence
E.g., "Mike, I will tell you something very important, but it's between you and me and the wall."

Have a lot on your plate—have a lot of things to do or worry about
E.g., Mary is a single mom and has a lot on the plate with three teen age sons, so I won't bother asking her to help me with my moving.

Lay your cards on the table—let someone know your feelings openly
E.g., he decided to lay his cards on the table and tell his girlfriend that he was not in love with her anymore.

Money under the table—money given secretly and often illegal
E.g., He paid the manager under the table so as to get a promotion.

Drink someone under the table—drink more alcohol than someone else without getting as drunk
E.g., at parties John always drinks his friends under the table.

On the fence—not able to decide
E.g., stop sitting on the fence. You must decide whose side you are on.

Lay something at someone's door—consider someone responsible for something
E.g., the accident was laid at the driver's door.

Brush up—quickly improve a skill, especially when you have not used one for a long time

E.g., I have to brush up my German before I visit my friends in Germany.

A needle in a haystack—a thing that is almost impossible to find

E.g., Searching for your penny in the garbage bin is like looking for a needle in a haystack.

Exercises

(1) Match the idioms with their definitions.

1. on the house
2. on the fence
3. nothing to write home about
4. a household name
5. talk to a brick wall
6. go through the roof
7. have the floor
8. a broken home
9. keep the home fires burning

a. a name everybody knows
b. speak but there is no answer
c. speak to a group
d. free
e. nothing special
f. keep things going
g. one's parents are divorced
h. not able to decide
i. become very angry

(2) Fill in the blanks with one of the following words:

daddy, closet, towel, sink, broom, pot, familiarity, blanket, houses, carpet

1. people who live in glass _____ should never throw stones
2. a watched _____ never boils
3. _____ breeds content
4. skeletons in the _____
5. throw in the _____
6. a wet _____
7. a new _____ sweeps clean
8. sweep under the _____
9. everything but the kitchen _____
10. sugar _____

(3) Is the speaker happy or unhappy when he/she:

1. has dinner on the house
2. is in the doghouse with someone
3. is called on the carpet
4. has skeletons in the closet
5. talks to a brick wall
6. has a night on the tiles
7. goes through the roof
8. gets up on the wrong side of the bed
9. has a lot on the plate
10. marries a sugar daddy

(4) Fill in the blanks with one of the following prepositions:

in, through, under, with, on, before, about, over

1. _____ the house
2. nothing to write home _____
3. call someone _____ the carpet
4. in the doghouse _____ someone
5. _____ the fence
6. go _____ the roof
7. sweep _____ the carpet
8. skeletons _____ the closet
9. get with someone like house _____ fire
10. a roof _____ your head.

(5) Complete the sentences so that they are true.

1. I had dinner on the house when _____
2. I was in the dog house with _____
3. I was once called on the carpet _____
4. _____ is really nothing to write home about
5. _____ might have skeletons in the closet

6. I went through the roof when _____
7. I went to the wall when _____
8. _____ came down on me.
9. I get on with _____ like house on fire

(6) Find someone who:

1. is in the doghouse with someone
2. got up on the wrong side of the bed
3. has thrown in the towel
4. is a wet blanket
5. has sometimes gone through the roof
6. has had dinner on the house

(7) Pair/group work: create your own situations using some of home idioms.

WORK

A workaholic—someone who is addicted to work and never stops to rest
E.g., Tim always works on the weekend and never takes vocations. His wife gets upset and calls him a workaholic.

Work like a dog—work very hard
E.g., Kelly has two jobs. She is working like a dog to make money to buy a house.

Work until you drop—work until you can't anymore
E.g., Tim is sixty-eight and never wants to retire. He plans to work until he drops.

Work one's way up the ladder—start at the bottom and work hard to get promoted higher and higher
E.g., my friend just got promoted again. She wants to work her way up the ladder until she becomes president of the company.

A labor of love—a kind of work that you really enjoy doing but it pays very little
E.g., It took her two years to write her book. It was a labor of love.

You reap what you sow—you get rewarded for good things you do and punished for bad things
E.g., Tom didn't study last school year and failed the exams—you reap what you sow.

Fall down on the job—fail to do something properly
E.g., Alex fell down on his job because he never finished his tasks.

Call it a day/night—stop working for the day or night
E.g., after working for almost twelve hours, they called it a day.

A blue-collar job—manual work

    E.g., my friend's husband has a blue-collar job. He works as a mechanic at Home Depot.

A white-collar job—clerical, professional work.

    E.g., Irma's son has a white-collar job. He works as an accountant at the National Bank.

A pink-collar job—types of jobs traditionally performed by women

    E.g., My cousin has a pink-collar job. She is a telephone operator at Rogers.

Girl/man Friday—female or male employee who does a variety of office jobs

    E.g., Susan is our girl Friday. She does different jobs in our office.

Get down to business— work seriously and not waste time

    E.g., let's get down to business; we have much to do.

Ambulance chaser ------ a lawyer who makes money by convincing people injured in accidents to claim money from the person who caused the accident

    E.g., Peterson is a famous ambulance chaser. That's how he makes his money.

A dead-end job—a job in which there is no opportunity to make progress or no chance to get better

    E.g., I would rather be unemployed than have a dead-end-job like yours.

Reach/hit a glass ceiling—that an invisible barrier prevents people, especially women, from career advancement

    E.g., The glass ceiling didn't let her rise to the managerial position.

Talk shop—talk about work
E.g., when I go out with my colleagues, I don't like to talk shop.

Work to rule—work only as much as is demanded by terms of employment, usually as a form of protest
E.g., while the union was at the table with the employer, we worked to rule.

Straw boss—a member of a work crew who acts as a supervisor
E.g., Jim is only a straw boss. He is dying to be in our manager's shoes.

In the works—being developed or planned
E.g., they say new work rules are in the works.

Skeleton staff—a small staff, just enough to do the job
E.g., their business is still small. They only have a skeleton staff at the moment.

A golden handshake—severance package
E.g., his grandfather was given a golden handshake when he retired after forty years with the company.

Throw a spanner in the works—do something that prevents an activity from succeeding
E.g., the death of the president threw a spanner in the works for our company.

Work against the clock—work very fast because you don't have enough time to do something
E.g., we have to work against the clock and finish this project. It's due tomorrow.

Snow job—misleading someone
> E.g., *Mathew was too late to class and was trying to give the teacher a snow job about the heavy traffic*

A plum job—a well-paid job that is not very hard
> E.g., *Alex is trying to find himself a plum job in Toronto.*

A cog in the machine—someone who plays a small part in a company or job
> E.g., *at the company she feels like just a cog in the machine, not really important.*

Moonlight—work as a second job, usually in the evening
> E.g., *most of my friends moonlight. Some of them deliver pizza.*

Bean counter—an accountant
> E.g., *Mary's husband is a bean counter. He does our income tax too.*

Busman's holiday—spending your free time doing the same kind of work you do in your regular job
> E.g., *Teaching her children French in the evening is a busman's holiday for her. She is a French teacher.*

Don't give up your day job—a way of telling someone that they are not doing a good job
> E.g., *Linda's husband asked her, "What do you think of my painting?"*
> *Linda said, "Hmm, well, don't give up your day job.*

Bad workers always blame their tools—when someone does a bad job and says that their equipment is to blame
> E.g., *When Elisabeth burned the cake, she said that her oven burns everything. Bad workers always blame their tools.*

Beggars can't be choosers—people who are in great need must accept anything offered to them
E.g., he accepted a low-paid job just to keep one foot in the door. Beggars can't be choosers.

The shoemaker's son always goes barefoot—a skillful person often fails to use his skills for himself or his family
E.g., Ann's father is a talented tailor, but Ann buys all her clothes. Her father is always too busy to make her clothes. The shoemaker's son always goes barefoot.

Get the sack—dismissed from work
E.g., He finally got the sack after being late almost every day.

Sweat blood—work very hard
E.g., He sweat blood to make his business a success.

By the sweat of your brow—work very hard
E.g., my neighbor has to win the bread by the sweat of her brow.

Monkey business—behavior which is deceitful, dishonest, or silly
E.g., The mother told her children to cut out the monkey business and start tidying up their rooms.

WORLD

On the top of the world—extremely happy
> E.g., when we were on vacations and enjoying life, we felt on the top of the world.

Think the world of someone—like and admire someone very much
> E.g., Elda is a caring mother, and her daughter Helen thinks the world of her.

Carry the world on one's shoulders—carry all the troubles of the world on one's shoulders
> E.g., What's the matter with you, Sam? You look like you are carrying the world on your shoulders!

The best of both worlds—the advantages of two different things at the same time
> E.g., My food is healthy and delicious. I have the best of both worlds.

Bottom drops (falls) out of somebody's world—someone loses the basis of happiness or hope
> E.g., when her husband passed away, the bottom dropped out of her world.

Come down in the world—lose one's social and financial position
> E.g., since he lost his job, Tom has really come down in the world.

Come up in the world—improve one's situation in life
> E.g., Since Mary got her new job, she has come up in the world.

Out of this world—very good or impressive
> E.g., the food in this restaurant is out of this world.

In a world of one's own—self-centered

E.g., John lives in a world of his own. He has very few friends.

It's a small world—express surprise when you unexpectedly meet someone you know in an unlikely place

E.g., I met my high school classmate in Canada. It's a small world.

Dead to the world—very tired, exhausted

E.g., I had such a tiring day. I am really dead to the world.

Not have a care in the world—unworried and carefree

E.g., Ann always acts like she doesn't have a care in the world.

For all the world—everything existing

E.g., I wouldn't sell my house for all the world.

It's not the end of the world—not so tragic

E.g., you failed the driving test, but you can try again. It's not the end of the world.

Think the world owes you a living—think you are worthy of being well supported or provided for

E.g., the world doesn't owe you a living. You should try to get a job yourself.

Worlds apart—very different in opinions

E.g., the two main political parties were worlds apart with their differing views on the tax increase law.

Have the world at your feet—be very successful and liked by a great number of people

E.g., When she got the first prize at Canadian Idol, she had the world at her feet.

A man/woman of the world—someone who has a lot of experience with life and people
E.g., My father is a man of the world, so I always ask him for advice.

Be/live in a dream world—someone hopes or thinks for things to happen when they are not likely to happen
E.g., Ann is living in a dream world if she thinks her manager will promote her in two months.

Be in another world—someone does not notice what is going on because they are thinking about something else
E.g., when the teacher called Cindy to answer the question, she was in another world and didn't know how to respond.

Tell the world—spread the word
E.g., I would not share my business plans with Sheryl. I do not trust her. She would tell the world.

Exercises

(1) Match the idioms with their definitions.

1. fall down on the job
2. out of this world
3. call it a day
4. a workaholic
5. get the sack
6. a plum job
7. on the top of the world
8. dead to the world
9. skeleton staff

a. a well-paid job that is not hard
b. be dismissed from work
c. stop working for the day
d. very tired
e. very small staff
f. to fail to do something properly
g. it's very good, impressive
h. extremely happy
i. someone who is addicted to work

(2) Finish the idioms with one of the following words:

collar, business, dead, girl, world, drop, boot, sow, love, shoulders

1. a labor of _____
2. you reap what you _____
3. a blue _____ job
4. give someone the _____
5. it's a small _____
6. carry the world on one's _____
7. a _____ Friday
8. a _____ end job
9. get down to _____
10. work until you _____

(3) Is the speaker happy or unhappy when he/she:

1. is a workaholic
2. calls it a day
3. works until they drop
4. works their way up the ladder
5. falls down on the job
6. is given the boot
7. is on top of the world
8. comes up in the world
9. does not have a care in the world
10. gets the best of both worlds

(4) Fill in the blanks with one of the following prepositions:

on, down, up, out, until, to

1. work _____ you drop
2. work one's way _____ the ladder
3. fall _____ on the job
4. work _____ rule
5. _____ of this world
6. _____ the top of the world
7. get _____ to business
8. come _____ in the world
9. carry the world _____ one's shoulders

(5) Complete the sentences so that they are true.

1. I worked like a dog when _____
2. _____ is a labor of love.
3. I worked until I dropped when _____
4. _____ is a workaholic.
5. _____ is a dead-end job.
6. I was on the top of the world when _____

7. _____ is out of this world.
8. I think the world of _____
9. The bottom fell out of my world when _____
10. _____ lives in a world of his own.

(6) Find someone who:

1. is a workaholic
2. has fallen down on his job
3. has a blue-collar job
4. was given the boot
5. is a girl Friday
6. has a dead-end job
7. is on the top of the world
8. has come up in the world
9. has worked his/her way up the ladder

(7) Pair/group work: create your own situations using some of the work and world idioms.

SCHOOL

Cut class—Skip going to class
E.g., he failed the course because he cut classes often.

Drop out—stop going to school.
E.g., he was no longer interested in his high school and dropped out.

Goof off—not study; hang around
E.g., George was goofing off last semester; that's why he failed in the exams.

Hit the books—study hard
E.g., it's time to hit the books because exams are coming.

Cook the books—make false records of a business, especially to take money illegally
E.g., the company accountant had been cooking the books for years and was sentenced to one year in jail.

Be in the good/bad books—be in or out of favor; someone is pleased or annoyed with you
E.g., Tom is in the good books of the manager. He will get a raise soon.

Read someone like a book—guess someone's thoughts or feelings
E.g., don't try to hide your problem. I can read you like a book.

Go by the book—work according to the rules
E.g., the new manager goes by the book. She wouldn't tolerate mistakes at work.

Have one's nose in a book—read all the time
E.g., My friend has got her nose in the book and never exercises.

Throw the book at someone—punish someone hard by giving the maximum penalties
E.g., The teacher threw the book at Bob for being late to class every day.

A bookworm—a person who reads a lot
E.g., My school friend Linda was a bookworm. She would not go anywhere with us. She enjoyed reading instead.

Cram for a test—study very hard for a test
E.g., I have a big test next week that I'll have to cram for.

Burn the midnight oil—work very hard until late at night
E.g., to become a doctor, you have to burn the midnight oil.

Pull an all-nighter—study all night
E.g., I have to pull an all-nighter because I have a very important test tomorrow.

A killer course—a very difficult class
E.g., this term I've taken up lexicology, a killer course; it is my hardest class.

Bomb a test—fail a test
E.g., he bombed his last test. He should have worked harder.

That's a turn up for the books—be very surprised
E.g., a Frenchman who doesn't like cheese and wine— that's a turn up for the books!

You could have knocked me down with a feather—very surprised
E.g., I bought only one lottery ticket and I won five thousand dollars. You could have knocked me down with a feather.

Teacher's pet—the teacher's favorite student

E.g., she always gets special treatment because she's the teacher's pet.

Cow college—a school where students study farming or agriculture

E.g., My neighbor is going to cow college next year because he wants to take over his dad's farm.

SPORTS

Have a lot on the ball—efficient; intelligent

E.g., we're very lucky to have Tom in our company. He has a lot on the ball.

Have a ball—have a great time

E.g., we really had a ball at the party last night; it was so much fun.

Start the ball rolling—begin an activity

E.g., The party began and I got up to dance just to start the ball rolling.

Keep the ball rolling—keep an activity going

E.g., it was getting late and we suggested ending the meeting. We couldn't keep the ball rolling anymore.

The ball is in your court—it's your turn to do something

E.g., The father helped his son buy a house and said, "Now, the ball is in your court. You must keep the house."

A ball of fire—a person who is full of energy and enthusiasm

E.g., his son is like a ball of fire. Look how he is all over the soccer in the field and loving it.

Carry the ball—be in charge

E.g., we needed someone who knows how to carry the ball for us, someone who knows how to get the job done.

Keep one's eye on the ball—remain alert to something happening

E.g., The teacher told his students to keep their eyes on the ball when the exam results would be posted.

Take the ball and run—continue in the right direction

E.g., Lisa gave me a good idea about my term plan. I think now I should take the ball and run.

Behind the eight ball—behind schedule; not coping very well

E.g., I am behind the eight ball in my English course. I need to study harder.

Play ball—work with other people in a helpful way so that everybody can get what they want

E.g., the three friends decided to open a business together. They played ball with each other and everyone was happy.

Beat the pants off—defeat someone by a large score

E.g., Irma plays chess very well. She'll beat the pants off you.

Heavyweight—a person of great importance or influence

E.g., Her husband's brother is a heavyweight in the provincial government.

Good sport—someone who does not boast if they win and does not complain if they lose

E.g., Ben always wins prizes, but he is such a good sport and he never shows off.

Soccer mom—a mother who spends a lot of time taking her children to activities

E.g., Nancy is a real soccer mom. She takes Max to soccer, piano lessons, and art classes.

Move the goalposts—change the rules

E.g., Our boss is always moving the goalposts. It's getting more and more difficult working for him.

Get your skates on—hurry up!

E.g., if you don't get your skates on, we'll be late.

Right off the bat—immediately

E.g., Ana found a wallet on the subway, and she returned it to the lost and found station right off the bat.

A level playing field—same conditions for everyone

E.g., Tom got a promotion, but Bill didn't. However, Tom's uncle is the boss, so it wasn't a level playing field.

PEOPLE

Every man jack—everyone

E.g., the company went bankrupt and they laid off every man jack.

A jack-of-all-trades—a person who can do many things

E.g., my friend is very lucky because her husband can fix everything in their house. He is a jack of all trades.

All work and no play makes Jack a dull boy—do not work too long and take time for recreation

E.g., Tom never goes out with his classmates. He would rather study than play even though they tell him, "All work and no play makes Jack a dull boy."

Bob's your uncle—you won't have a problem, everything will be fine, something will be successful

E.g., I gave Mary the instructions how to make a cheese pie and then I said, Put it in the oven for thirty minutes and Bob's your uncle, it will be ready when your kids get home.

Don't know him from Adam—I have never met him; I don't know who he is

E.g., he says he knows me, but I don't know him from Adam.

Sophie's choice—accept what is offered or you get nothing

E.g., Mary was mad at her daughter for not eating the soup. Mary asked her to eat it or she would get nothing else. It was Sophie's choice.

Johnny-on-the -spot—someone who is always ready to help when needed

E.g., I got up late and I needed a ride this morning, and there my son was, Johnny-on-the-spot who gave me a ride to school.

Let George do it—wait for someone to do it
E.g., he never takes the initiative to fix something. His attitude is let George do it.

Smart aleck—conceited; pretending to know everything
E.g., you should sometimes listen to what other people tell you. Don't be a smart aleck.

"Mr. and Mrs. Smith"—is a popular way of remaining anonymous (like when booking a hotel)
E.g., When Mary was dating her husband, they used to go to the same hotel and signed as "Mr. and Mrs. Smith".

Rob Peter to pay Paul—satisfy one need by creating another
E.g., don't use your rent money to make a car payment. You are robbing Peter to pay Paul.

A Darby and Joan—a faithful, loving, old married couple
E.g., My grandparents were a Darby and Joan. They lived a long life together and never disappointed each other.

Achilles' heel—weak point
E.g., not being able to use a computer was his Achilles' heel.

The real McCoy—genuine, real
E.g., the jeweler examined Mira's ring and said the diamond was the real McCoy.

Johnny-come-lately—someone who joins in something late
E.g., we've been waiting for thirty minutes. Why should some Johnny-come-lately tell us what to do?

Lead the life of Riley—live in luxury
E.g., if I had one million dollars, I would lead the life of Riley and indulge.

Pandora's box—do something that unintentionally causes a lot of problems

E.g., don't open a Pandora's box and complicate the situation.

Keep up with the Joneses—try for the same nice things that other people have

E.g., Keeping up with the Joneses his getting harder and harder in my neighborhood. Let's move to a new area.

Every Tom, Dick, and Harry—anyone

E.g., I thought they would select the best candidates for the job, but every Tom, Dick, and Harry got hired.

A Freudian slip—a mistake which shows an unconscious thought, usually in speaking

E.g., Amanda got mad at her boyfriend when he said to her, "I wish you were her," instead of "I wish you were here."

A doubting Thomas—someone who will not believe something unless he has seen it himself

E.g., don't be a doubting Thomas. You should believe me this time.

The Midas touch the ability to make a lot of money

E.g., Harry is a successful businessman. He has the Midas touch.

A good Samaritan—one who helps those in need

E.g., a good Samaritan paid my bus fare when I lost my wallet.

An Aladdin's cave—a place where interesting and useful objects can be found

E.g., Robert's attic looks like an Aladdin's cave; I found so many cool things.

A Jekyll and Hyde—someone who shows two opposite sides of his character

E.g., Dora married Jim but unfortunately she figured out that he was a Jekyll and Hyde. He has showed his cruel side sometimes.

A Mrs. Grundy—a person who thinks they are better than everyone else

E.g., Margaret can't stand her mother-in-law for being so critical and priggish. Everyone calls her mother-in-law a Mrs. Grundy.

A nosey Parker—someone who is too interested in other people's business and is very inquisitive

E.g., I didn't invite my next door neighbor to my party as she would start asking everyone about their lives and business. She is just a nosey Parker.

A Debbie downer—a person who always has something negative to say and brings other people down

E.g., Margaret was not invited to the party because she is a Debbie downer.

Pollyanna—someone who is always cheerful and thinks something good is coming

E.g., Nancy is always a pleasure to be with. She would cheer you up and make you feel happy any time she is around you. She is a real Pollyanna.

Hobson's choice—accept what is offered or you get nothing

E.g., mother told her daughter to eat the soup or she would get nothing else. It was Hobson's choice.

Jack and Jill—a party held for a couple soon to be married to which both men and women are invited

E.g., Tom and Helen are getting married next week and they are having a Jack and Jill party this weekend.

Happy as Larry—very happy

E.g., The holidays were good. We could be happy as Larry if we had no rain.

Cinderella—a person or thing that has been ignored and deserves to get more attention

E.g., for years radio has been the Cinderella of the media world; it should receive more attention.

Before you say Jack Robinson—do something very quickly

E.g., I promise I'll finish my homework before you say Jack Robinson.

Mister/Miss Right—the right person for a marriage

E.g., everyone thought Mara had finally found her Mister Right.

Nervous Nellie—a woman who worries for unnecessary matters

E.g., her friend Linda is a nervous Nellie, worrying about everything.

Murphy's law------ if anything can go wrong, it will

E.g. I am going to New York tomorrow, in spite of the news that there will be a blizzard.
But I remember, Murphy's Law.

COUNTRY

Go Dutch—share the cost to pay one's bill
E.g., When we go out for lunch with my friends, we prefer to go Dutch.

In Dutch—in trouble
E.g., Tom is in Dutch with his parents for his low grades.

Meet one's Waterloo—meet one's final challenge, be defeated by someone stronger
E.g., She was doing fine as our supervisor, but she met her Waterloo when she got the manager's position.

Fiddle while Rome burns—someone spends time on unimportant things when they have very serious problems to deal with
E.g., everyone was worried about her little brother's illness, but she was watching a movie on TV. Fiddle while Rome burns.

Rome was not built in a day—it takes a long time to be successful
E.g., her husband just started a business and wants to make millions right away, but Rome was not built in a day.

When in Rome, do as the Romans do—one should behave in the same way that the local people behave
E.g., everyone in my new company dresses so formally, and I guess I should do the same. When in Rome, do as Romans do.

All roads lead to Rome—there are many ways to reach the goal
E.g., Jane was solving the math problem in a different way than Tom, but they both managed to solve it—all roads lead to Rome.

It's Greek to me—difficult to understand
> *E.g., I don't understand what you are trying to tell me—it's Greek to me.*

Send someone to Coventry—refuse to associate with someone as a punishment
> *E.g., We sent Sarah to Coventry for being rude to all of us.*

Russian roulette—an action that might be very dangerous and risk your life
> *E.g., windsurfing in this terrible storm is like playing Russian roulette.*

Not for all the tea in China—Never, not even if you gave me everything
> *E.g., I wouldn't go back to him, not for all the tea in China.*

American as apple pie—very American
> *E.g., Country music is as American as apple pie.*

Black Russian---- a cocktail made from coffee liquor and vodka
> *E.g. After he had three shots of Black Russian, he got drunk as a skunk.*

Exercises

(1) Match the idioms with their definitions.

1.	have a lot on the ball	a.	skip going to class
2.	carry the ball	b.	study hard until it's late
3.	cut class		
4.	hit the books	c.	genuine
5.	pull an all-nighter	d.	in trouble
6.	a bookworm	e.	share the cost
7.	the real McCoy	f.	study hard
8.	go Dutch	g.	it's difficult to understand
9.	it's Greek to me		
10.	in Dutch	h.	intelligent
		i.	someone who always studies
		j.	be in charge

(2) Complete the idioms with one of the following words:

oil, Rome, heel, waterloo, pay, aleck, book, box, teacher

1. Throw the _____ at someone
2. smart _____
3. rob Peter to _____ Paul
4. Achilles' _____
5. Pandora's _____
6. fiddle while _____ burns
7. all roads lead to _____
8. meet one's _____
9. burn the midnight _____
10. _____'s pet

(3) Find someone who:

1. cuts class
2. drops out
3. has a killer course
4. bombs a test
5. is in good books of his teacher
6. has a friend who is a smart aleck
7. leads the life of Riley
8. is in Dutch with someone
9. is behind the eight ball
10. has a lot on the ball

(4) Complete the idioms with one of the following prepositions:

out, on, off, with, to, for, in, by, behind

1. keep one's eye _____ the ball
2. beat the pants _____
3. _____ the eight ball
4. drop _____
5. goof _____
6. go _____ the book
7. in Dutch _____ someone
8. all roads lead _____ Rome
9. cram _____ a test
10. Rome was not built _____ a day

(5) Complete the sentences so that they are true.

1. We had a ball when _____
2. I was behind the eight ball when _____
3. I carried the ball for _____
4. _____ had to drop out when _____
5. I had to hit the books when _____

6. _____ was a killer course.
7. _____ is a bookworm.
8. _____ is a jack-of-all-trades.
9. _____ is Johnny-on-the-spot.
10. We usually go Dutch with _____

(6) Find someone who:

1. has sent someone to Coventry
2. has a lot on the ball
3. is behind the eight ball
4. has dropped out
5. goofs off
6. has his nose in a book
7. is the teacher's pet
8. goes by the book
9. leads a life of Riley

(7) Pair/group work: create your own situations using some of the school, sports, people, or country idioms.

TRAVEL

In the same boat—in the same unpleasant or difficult situation

E.g., *Martha and Sam are in the same boat: unemployed and divorced.*

Miss the boat—don't act in time so you miss the opportunity.

E.g., *I managed to fax my application for the job before the deadline. I nearly missed the boat.*

Rock the boat—upset a pleasant situation and cause trouble

E.g., *Greg and his wife are quite happy together, but her nosey mother is rocking the boat by interfering.*

Backseat driver—an annoying person who gives unwanted advice to others.

E.g., *George told his wife to stop being a backseat driver while he is driving.*

In the driver's seat—in charge of things

E.g., *things are changing for the better in our company since Irma has been in the driver's seat.*

Sunday driver—a slow driver who holds up the traffic by enjoying the view

E.g., *That Sunday driver is holding up traffic. We are getting late for the meeting.*

Drive someone up the wall—annoy or irritate someone

E.g., *The noise outside is driving me up the wall.*

My way or the highway—either accept what I say or quit the project

E.g., *When his manager said, "My way or the highway," Greg had to accept it. He didn't want to leave.*

Drita Skilja

Highways and byways—take large and small roads to visit every part of a country
E.g., Peter travelled the highways and byways, enjoying every part of his grandparents' country.

Hit the road—begin a journey
E.g., we had a long trip to Montreal, so we hit the road at 5:00 a.m.

One for the road—the last drink before one decides to go home
E.g., we decided to have one for the road and then go home.

Take someone for a ride—deceive or cheat someone
E.g., that coat was on sale, but he charged me regular price. He took me for a ride.

Fifth wheel—their presence is unnecessary or useless
E.g., everyone in the party had a role except me. I felt like a fifth wheel.

Wheels fall off—the situation gets out of control; things start to go wrong
E.g., when Victor started to cut classes, the wheels fell off his schooling.

Asleep at the wheel—someone is not attentive enough, especially when vigilance is necessary
E.g., the bank security guard was asleep at the wheel when the bank was robbed.

Put the pedal to the metal—go faster
E.g., Ben, let's put the pedal to the metal. I don't want to be late for the meeting.

- 182 -

Any port in a storm—a solution you accept since it is the only choice, but in normal circumstances you would not accept it

E.g., *Rita doesn't like her job, but this is the only one she can get at the moment. Any port in the storm, you know?*

Sail close to the wind—do something dangerous; take risks

E.g., *I think driving at 120 kilometers per hour is sailing close to the wind. Let's slow down.*

Sail through—succeed in doing a test or procedure without difficulty

E.g., *Jeff studied so hard for the TOEFL test and sailed through it.*

Ships that pass in the night—people who you meet briefly and may not meet again

E.g., *she fell in love with someone she met on the plane and never saw him again, like ships that pass in the night.*

Live out of a suitcase—someone who travels a lot

E.g., *Ann is tired of her job, as it involves so much travelling that she lives out of a suitcase.*

Train of thought—a sequence of connected ideas

E.g., *the telephone ring broke my train of thought.*

On the wagon—no longer drinking alcohol

E.g., *we were all surprised at the party that Allen had nothing to drink. He said he was on the wagon.*

Exercises

(1) Match the idioms with the definitions.

1.	rock the boat	a.	large and small roads
2.	hit the road	b.	not sufficiently attentive
3.	train of thought	c.	no longer drinking alcohol
4.	on the wagon	d.	upset a stable situation
5.	sail through	e.	begin a journey
6.	highway and byways	f.	a sequence of ideas
7.	in the driver's seat	g.	succeed in doing something
8.	asleep at the wheel	h.	in charge

(2) Complete the idioms with one of the following words:

boat, wheel, ships, highway, wind, backseat, driver,

1. Sail close to the _____
2. Miss the _____
3. My way or the _____
4. _____ that pass in the night
5. _____ driver
6. fifth _____
7. Sunday _____

(3) Are you happy or unhappy when:

1. you miss the boat
2. someone drives you up the wall
3. you feel like a fifth wheel
4. you live out of a suitcase
5. you sail through

(4) Fill in the blanks.

1. _____ the same boat
2. drive someone _____ the wall
3. put the pedal _____ the metal
4. any port _____ a storm
5. take someone _____ a ride
6. live _____ of a suitcase
7. wheels fall _____
8. asleep _____ the wheel

(5) Complete the sentences so that they are true for you.

1. I missed the boat when _____
2. I sailed close to the wind when _____
3. I felt like a fifth wheel when _____
4. I sailed through when _____
5. I am in the same boat with _____
6. The last time I hit the road was _____

(6) Find someone who:

1. is on the wagon
2. lives out of a suitcase
3. has sailed close to the wind
4. has sailed through
5. has missed the boat
6. is in the same boat with you

(7) Pair/group work: create your own situations using some of the travel idioms.

MUSIC

Face the music—accept the consequences of your mistakes

E.g., Anna broke her father's car window, and when she got home, she had to face the music.

Music to your ears—what you hear is what you want or what makes you happy

E.g., Trafford's decision to publish my book was music to my ears.

Chin music—meaningless talk

E.g., I would not like to go to my neighbor's party and get tired of their chin music.

Elevator music—popular instrumental music usually played in doctor offices or while on hold on the telephone

E.g., I am tired of the elevator music when I call the doctor and they put me on hold.

Ring a bell—something sounds familiar but you don't remember exactly what

E.g., Cathy Smith? This name rings a bell, but I can't remember her.

For a song—something that costs very little money

E.g., my friend got a car for a song just because it had a broken mirror.

Play it by ear— improvise; do/say things according to the circumstances

E.g., I don't know what to say in my speech at my friend's wedding. I'll just play it by ear.

Play second fiddle to someone—accept you have a lower position than someone else

E.g., when his son became his company manager, he decided to quit. He didn't like to play second fiddle to his son.

As fit as a fiddle—in excellent physical condition

E.g., After getting the medication and drinking a lot of fluids, the doctor told him he was as fit as a fiddle.

Drum into someone's head—teach something repeatedly

E.g., our parents drummed into our head the value of education.

Jazz up—add something to try to improve; to make it more stylish

E.g., Nancy wore a nice red belt to jazz up her black dress.

All that jazz—everything of this kind

E.g., when he left her, she said he was a liar, unfaithful, and all that jazz.

Strike a false/right note—do something inappropriate/ appropriate

E.g., He struck a false note when he arrived at the interview late.

Sound like a broken record—repeat the same thing over and over

E.g., He sounds like a broken record when he complains about his boss over and over.

Change your tune—change your mind/heart

E.g., Mary was deeply in love with Bill, but she changed her tune when she noticed he was rude.

Call the tune—make all the important decisions

E.g., It's our manager who calls the tune in our company.

Sing a different tune—change your attitude/opinion about something

E.g., they didn't believe him, but when they realized he was innocent, they sang a different tune.

Blow the whistle—give information or report who is responsible for an illegal activity

E.g., the neighbors blew the whistle on the burglars by calling the police.

Exercises

(1) Match the idioms with the definitions.

1.	rings a bell	a.	healthy
2.	all that jazz	b.	meaningless talk
3.	change your tune	c.	it sounds familiar
4.	face the music	d.	accept the
5.	as fit as a fiddle		consequences
6.	call the tune	e.	all that stuff
7.	strike the right note	f.	do the right thing
8.	chin music	g.	make all the decisions
		h.	change your opinion

(2) Complete the idioms:

1. _____ into someone's head
2. face the _____
3. elevator _____
4. sing a different _____
5. sounds like a broken _____
6. blow the _____
7. play second _____
8. play it by _____

(3) Are you happy or unhappy when:

1. you are as fit as a fiddle
2. you strike a false note
3. you listen to chin music
4. you face the music
5. you buy something for a song
6. something is drummed into your head

(4) Fill in the blanks.

1. _____ a song
2. drum _____ someone's head
3. music _____ your ear
4. play it _____ ear
5. jazz something _____

(5) Complete the sentences so that they are true for you.

1. I feel as fit as a fiddle when _____
2. I stroke the right note when _____
3. I stroke a false note when _____
4. I played it by ear when _____
5. _____ was drummed into my head.
6. I faced the music when _____
7. I bought _____ for a song.
8. _____ was music to my ears.

(6) Find someone who:

1. has bought something for a song
2. is as fit as a fiddle
3. has struck a false note
4. has played it by the ear
5. has changed their tune about someone
6. has jazzed something up

(7) Pair/group work: create your own situations using some of the music idioms.

REFERENCES

Broukal, Milada. 1994. *Idioms for Every Day Use*. Chicago, Illinois: National Textbook Company.

Dixon, Robert J. 1983. *Essential Idioms in English*. Englewood Cliffs, New Jersey: Prentice Hall, Inc.

Feare, Ronald E. 1980. *Practice with Idioms*. New York, NY: Oxford University Press.

Goldman, Lorraine. 1985. *Moving Ahead with Idioms*. New York, NY: Minerva Books, Ltd.

Huizenga, Jann. 2000. *Can You Believe It?* New York, NY: Oxford University Press.

Magnuson, Wayne. 2001. *English Idioms*. Calgary, Alberta: Prairie House Books.

McCaig, Isabel R., and Martin H. Manser. 1990. *A Learner's Dictionary of English Idioms*. London: Oxford University Press.

Wright, John. 2002. *Idioms Organizer*. Boston, MA: Heinle.

Spears, Richard A. 1999. *Phrases and Idioms*. New York, NY: McGraw-Hill Companies, Inc.

ABOUT THE AUTHOR

Drita Skilja has been an English-as-a-second-language (ESL) teacher for about thirty five years. She was born in Albania and graduated from Tirana University as an English teacher. She has been an Ontario TESL (Teaching English as a Second Language) certified ESL instructor with the Toronto District School Board since then. She is married and has two sons and three adorable grandchildren. She loves teaching, reading, socializing, and classic movies.

ABOUT THE BOOK

This collection of 1,001 English idioms is a highly useful tool for students of the English language. The idioms are divided into twenty relevant topics: food, body, animals, money, comparisons, nature, colors, numbers, love and war,.. and.., clothes, home, school, work, world, sports, people, country, travel and music. Each unit consists of a wide selection of idioms that are explained and used in examples to clearly illustrate the true point of each idiom. Each unit is followed by practice exercises to help the students reinforce the use and meaning of the idioms. This book is also a reference tool for teachers of English as a second language.